Love "THEM," Love YOU More

8 Ways to Re-Define Your Priorities Of Health As A Successful CEO Mom

TOYE PENNY

Creator Of The Love You More Method™

LOVE "THEM," LOVE YOU MORE. Copyright 2021 by Toye Penny. All rights reserved. No part of this publication may be reproduced, distributed, or transmitted in any form or by any means, including photocopying, recording, or other electronic or mechanical methods, without the prior written permission of the publisher, except in the case of brief quotations embodied in critical reviews and certain other noncommercial uses permitted by copyright law.

For permission requests, write to the publisher, addressed "Attention: Permissions Co-ordinator," 205 N. Michigan Avenue, Suite #810, Chicago, IL 60601. 13th & Joan books may be purchased for educational, business or sales promotional use. For information, please email the Sales Department at sales@13thandjoan.com.

Printed in the U. S. A.
First Printing, October 2020

Library of Congress Cataloging-in-Publication Data has been applied for.

ISBN: 978-1-953156-05-1

Love "THEM,"
Love YOU More

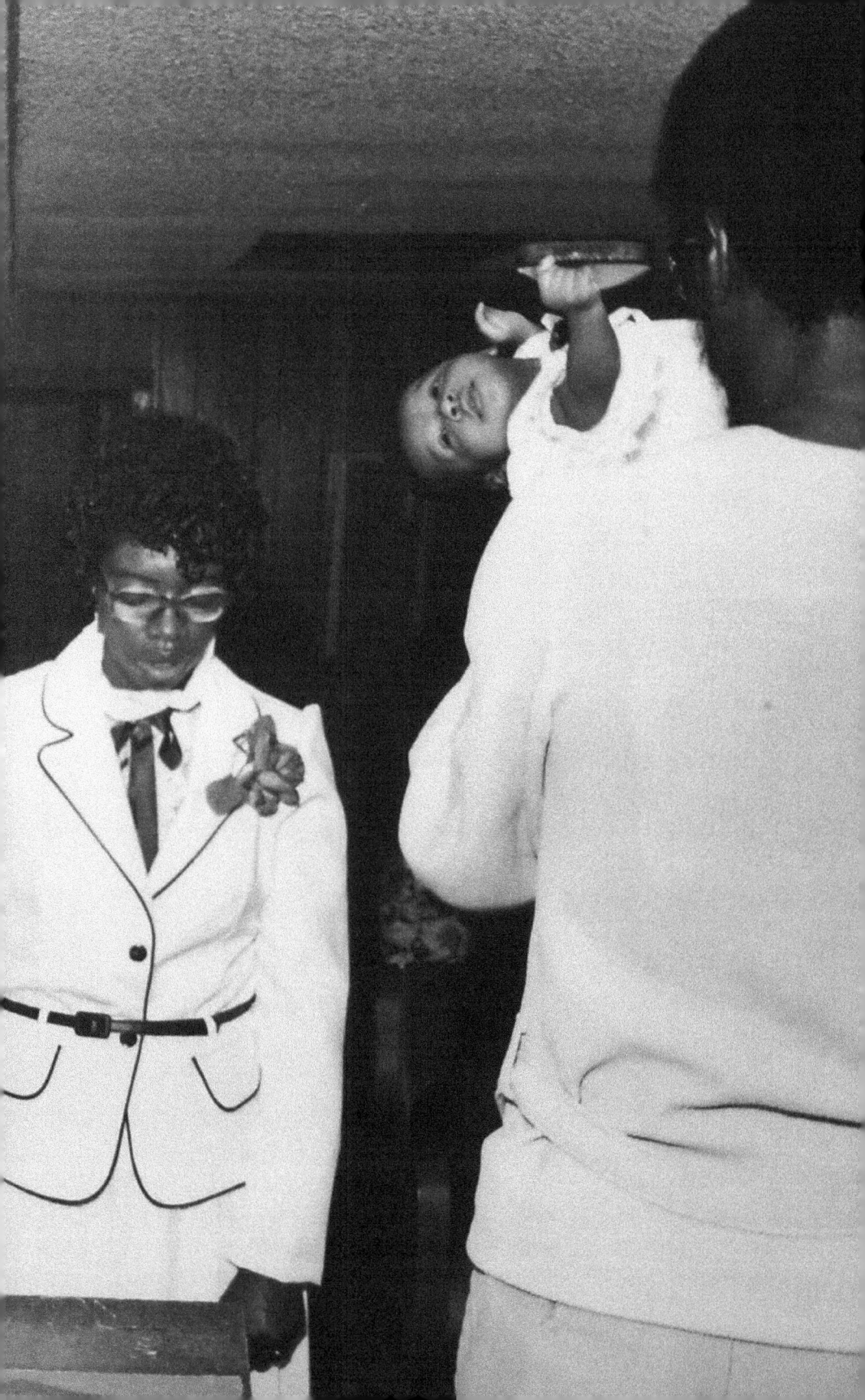

Dedication

To my mother, who was named Sandra. One of the reasons I do what I do is for you. My whole business model represents the CEO mom who couldn't quite find her healthy balance in life. Even though you left this earth when I was only nine years old, I KNOW that you loved me. When I saw this picture with the tears streaming down your face, it confirmed it all and reassured me that I was loved. Thanks for taking the time to give me back to God when you weren't sure of how things were going to go yourself. That was the BEST decision you made for me and I am forever grateful. I can't even begin to imagine how you felt once you knew your life was ending and you knew that you had to leave this earth without me. Well, I am picking up where you left off. For every broken dream, unhealthy meal, relationship that didn't feed your soul, all the late nights, not knowing what you were going to do next and for all the things you weren't taught…this is for you. Thanks so much for giving birth to me and trusting that God would see me through, He absolutely did. I'm so very proud of your efforts. I made it, and honestly, so did you…Love, your daughter Toye.

To this beautiful baby…Toye, If I knew then what life was going to take you through, I would hold you super tight and tell you to hang on because it's about to be a bumpy ride. I would also tell you not to worry, because everything will fall together in its place at the right time. Toye, you are a strong, courageous woman. You have been through so much and are still standing. For that, I am proud of you. Thank you for honoring yourself and wanting to encourage other women to do the same. Thank you for living life and deciding that loving you more was going to take you to the next level. Thank you for pushing through when you wanted to give up. Thank you for being you and opening up and sharing your true story with the world. Thank you for setting an example for others around you even when you felt like you weren't one. You are a great woman, wife, mother, health strategist, and so much more. Continue to stay connected to your source so that the gifts and talents He gave you will forever bless others. I know that your mother would be so proud of everything that you are. Love You More, Toye.

Acknowledgements

To my Heavenly Father who has been with me all along... Wow! God, you are so good! Thank you for keeping me. Thank you for helping me use all of life's broken pieces for your glory. Thank you for peace in the midst of the storm. Even though there were days when I left you, you never left me. When I didn't think of you, you thought of me. When I wasn't looking out for myself, Lord you were looking out for me. Thank you for the closed doors that no one could open and thank you for the open doors that no one can shut. Thank you for your many blessings, and I will continue to trust you through my life's journey. I ask that whoever you send to purchase and read this book, that they are touched in some way and are encouraged to seek you and live a healthier lifestyle by loving themselves as you love us. Amen.

To my WONDERFUL husband who supports me no matter what... Thank you so much. I thank God for you everyday. Words cannot express how grateful I am to have you in my life. You are my rock, my supporter, my encourager, my everything. AND, you spoil me to pieces. Thanks for all of the spa days, the "me" times, getting up in the middle of the night with the kiddos, the shoulder rubs, nourishing meals when I wasn't able to, cleaning the house and so much more. You are a great husband to me and an AMAZING father to our children. Honestly, I look at how you interact with our girls and can only imagine what that is like for them. As you know, I didn't have that example, so for them to have what I didn't have…I am beyond grateful. I observe the way they look at you in your eyes, run to you when you come home, and bypass me to get to you when things are broken and need to be fixed. While I sit and watch, I'm like… Wow! How beautiful is that? I pray that you continue to grow within Christ and yourself and He uses you to become an even greater example of what a man, husband, and father should look like. Thanks for being by my side, Penny.

To my beautiful daughters… I thank God everyday for you all. From my oldest daughter all the way to my baby daughter. Tavia, I pray that this book gives you the encouragement you need to go after your dreams. Don't stop for no one, surround yourself with positive, supportive people who are already where you want to be in life and soak up as much knowledge as you can. Search within yourself to find your God given purpose and Run With It! Summer, my hopes are that this book will one day give you the courage to stand even when no one is paying attention. You are so smart and have so much pizzazz, I just know you are going to take over the world one day. Kenza, (my baby girl) I dream that this book will help you tap into and discover the power that you hold, so you can use it to change lives. Your smile, your courage and your strength is going to take you places. I just know it. This is for you all. You are the future of this world and I am determined to break chains and leave a legacy of health, joy, and wholeness within your lives and your children's lives and your children's, children's lives and so on. We all have an assignment on this earth, and I pray that you all find yours, so go, go, go! Love, Mommy.

To Branny...Thanks so much for raising me into adulthood and building a foundation of love, God, and compassion within me. I remember all of those late nights of talks, showing me how to thread a needle, and cooking fish from the butcher shop up the street. I also remember the drop offs to the Kirk Franklin concerts, the cries for me to meet my "Jack" from the movie Titanic, and the rushed mornings trying to get to church on time. Thanks for being a grandmother/mom to me and teaching me my work ethic. Thanks for coming over and sitting with the kids while I write this awesome book for others to enjoy. Your works are not in vain and I am so grateful to have such a wonderful, inspirational, positive, encouraging grandmother like yourself. I pray MANY blessings upon your life and may you continue to inspire others to be great individuals.

To all others who helped me make this book a success... Cameron from Grand Homes, thanks for saying yes to my request. Congrats on your wedding and I pray many years to you and your new bride. Cheers to your marriage! Rodrick Connor, my photographer, thanks for all of these wonderful photos and spending time with me to make them right. You rock. Renee, my therapist, girl...thanks for pouring into me on a weekly basis for two.whole.years. And still counting! Thanks for going over photos and helping me brainstorm what should go on the front cover. Thanks for crying with me, helping me embrace and heal my brokenness, and being that confidant in my circle. You are more than just my therapist, you are a friend. To my business mentor, Kelly O'Neil and my PBI family, thanks for being winners in my circle and demonstrating winning on a daily basis. Thanks for being my eagles to soar with. I love you guys. To all my family and friends who have supported me, Every. Step. Of. The. Way (you know who you are). Thanks so much for being my support system. Without you, this process would've been a lot more difficult. I'm grateful. Love you all dearly.

> "I found myself feeding my daughter a chili cheese dog and some Dorito chips for dinner while I scarfed down four slices of cold pizza that I was too tired to warm up. It was then I realized that there needed to be a shift. An unhealthy lifestyle and unbalanced meals could no longer be our story."

The Beginning...

The moment when you're a mom with a career trying to maintain it all. You get home from the office and all you want to do is take off your clothes and hop in the bed. But, nope...there's other things to do. I call it, "work after work." Things like doing the dishes, making bottles or helping the kids with homework, monitoring curfew time, laundry, cooking dinner, bath time, last minute water requests before bed, snuggle time with hubby and a long list FULL of other things. And, then... When everyone is finally asleep (and in the house safe and sound), you have a little time for yourself, but Gee Golly... you're too tired to do anything, so you just go to bed. Whew!

This was me about 7 short years ago. But let's take a trip... rewind the hands of time a bit, and go back BEFORE I became that "off balanced, cold pizza eating, CEO mom."

When I was about 5 years old, my mom (who was single) was diagnosed with Lupus. While I was too young to know how it affected her, I do remember the impact it had on me. I remember my mother being in and out of the hospital and I stayed with my godparents most of the time. After my 6th birthday, my mother asked me to run in the grocery store to get a few things and unknowingly, I sort of became the one doing the grocery shopping and cooking for our household. There was a grocery store across the street from our apartment and my mom would give me a blank check and I would fill it out at the time of checkout. I know you're thinking… "that's a lot of responsibility for a 7 year old." But, the truth is, I handled it well.

Once I returned home from the grocery store, I would, then, unpack the groceries and start to prepare dinner. Now, I don't know how old you are, but back in the 80's there was a popular chicken mix called, "Shake 'N' Bake," and that was my go-to meal that I loved to make.

I would take the chicken legs (my favorite part of the chicken), place them in a ziplock bag along with the bake mix, and shake away, until the chicken was fully coated in this bready, floury looking stuff. Then, I'd take the chicken out of the bag, place it on a baking sheet, and put in the oven. While the chicken was baking, I would make canned green beans and canned corn and top the meal off with a popular orange drink called, "Tang." It was an orange powder mixture that you add water and sugar to, sort of like Kool-Aid. On some days, I would even invite family members over and cook for them. I started to become known for my famous "Shake 'N' Bake" chicken.

By the time I was 8 years old, my mother had fallen more ill than when she was first diagnosed; and I was spending an even greater amount of time with my godparents, so my cooking responsibilities were taken away. They were my caretakers, so they cooked delicious food for me, helped me with my homework, and loved me like I was their own. They even bought me the Little Mermaid doll and cassette tape and let me sing at the top of my lungs. I really loved being with them, and even though I loved cooking those "Shake 'N' Bake" meals, there was a sense of security that I felt being  with my godparents; something that every child needs. I used to lie in bed at night thinking, *I would love to be adopted by them.* But, it was just a thought.

One particular day, I was sitting at the kitchen table with my godmother, holding a conversation (I loved to talk), and the adoption topic came up. Since it was just a thought, I figured I'd see if it could become a reality, so I told her that I wanted to be adopted by her. She thought that was a lovely idea and felt the same way, but advised me not to tell my mother because that would make her angry and she would come and get me. Later that evening, my mother called to check in on me, as she always did, and the first moment of silence there was, I asked her. I wanted to know if it was okay for my godmother to adopt me. She told me that we would talk about it later.

The next morning, my mom sent a relative to come and get me. I was devastated. I remember crying for my godmother for hours. The next thing I know, they asked me if I wanted to go spend a night over one of my uncle's house (my mom's brother), and that's where I ended up living, along with his wife, and two other children. My mom had been looking elsewhere for me to live all along. About a month after I turned 9 years old, my uncle picked me up from school and told me he had to talk to me. We pulled up to the house and we walked outside, and he sat me down on the curb. He, then, went on to tell me that my mom had passed away. Turns out she was on the list to get a kidney transplant and didn't make it in time. Her kidneys had failed. I didn't know how to feel; however, I do remember my heart feeling like it was beating through my chest and falling to the ground.

I felt like I had lost my best friend. If only she would've taken better care of herself, we wouldn't be where we are now. I wouldn't feel like this and I wouldn't be living with my uncle and his family. I didn't know where to go from there, but what I did know was, I had to keep going. I missed her already, and it had just happened. It hurt and it still does occasionally. That night, I had a dream that seemed like a nightmare. My mom was calling my name in an unknown apartment complex. As I was walking, trying to find her, I was looking through all of the apartments because the doors were open. She kept calling my name and I kept walking towards her voice, calling hers. I finally came upon one door, and there she was, rocking in a rocking chair, telling me to come here. When I came to her she started decaying and trying to scratch my face up with very long nails, and all I was trying to do was hug her. Then, I woke up. I was sweaty, breathing hard, and crying; and no one was there to hold me. This is when I REALLY started to miss her, because she would always hold me whenever I had bad dreams. When her funeral date arrived, I was completely numb. Numb to the fact that she was gone, numb to the fact of everything that happened, and numb to the fact that this was my reality. I remember walking up to her casket and giving her a kiss on her cheek. She was so beautiful. When I walked away, I felt cold inside. I was lost without her, but I had to keep going. When we got to her burial, we put her down in the ground…and that was it. I told myself that I was going to put it in the back of my mind and move on. And, that's what I did.

LIVING WITH MY UNCLE

Living with my uncle and his family wasn't easy. They were a blended family, and adding me in the mix made it a little more difficult. I constantly felt out of place and not "at home." My aunt-in-law (my uncle's wife), had a daughter who was one year my senior, and a son who was two years my junior. We got along pretty well, and even though we weren't brothers and sisters, it sort of felt like we were. I mean…we were kids.

My uncle worked a lot to provide for the family, so I didn't see him as much. He was gone before I woke up, and oftentimes, came in after we were gone to bed. Dinner was always made by my uncle's wife, as we weren't allowed in the kitchen to cook. Most of the time, our meals consisted of things like T.V. dinner trays, oatmeal, meatloaf, chicken and dumplings, and baked chicken. Nothing spectacular, but I can say, "healthy meals" were far from their minds. After dinner, we were made to do the dishes and we had assigned days to do them. If we didn't do our chores, we would miss our allowance for the week. One afternoon, after I got home from school, my aunt-in-law told me to hop in the car cause she was taking me to McDonald's. We drove for about 30 minutes before we got there, and when we arrived, I was sent off to play in the playground while she met with a lady. I didn't know the lady, but I did see that they were going over some paperwork together and the two of them laughed a bit, so I thought they were friends. (Remember where we left off, because I'll come back to this particular part of my story in a bit.)

Being with my uncle and his family was beginning to get frustrating to me. I started missing my mom a lot and I had no one to really talk to about it. I couldn't talk to him because he was always gone, and I felt as though he couldn't relate to me; and I definitely couldn't talk to his wife because she didn't converse with me much. Nine o'clock was our set bedtime. When my uncle would come home (usually around ten), I would hear them argue over me and my well-being. My uncle would argue with his wife over things like, getting her daughter's hair done and not mine, my clothes not looking decent enough, or not spending my social security money in the right places. I began to start thinking that it was my fault that they were arguing and I was making things worse. This made my self-esteem really low.

By the time I was twelve years old, we had bought a new house and I had transferred schools. Being in middle school was a whole new world for me, and I really enjoyed the company that it kept. I was in choir and cheerleading, and both of them, I was

really good at. I have always loved to sing (my mother did, too) and the girly athlete in me just wouldn't let me be ineffectual at cheerleading, so I took them both really serious. Plus, they were extra curricular activities and it was expected of me to keep my grades up. On the weekends, I would go over my grandmother's (my mom's mother) house where I had about six cousins my age, and they would come over to spend time with me. We would do things like cook, make tents, go exploring in the creek behind her house, sing, sew clothes and host fashion shows. We always kept busy and got into so much. My grandmother was a seamstress and she taught us how to thread a needle and sew. It was always so much fun over there; I got to live a little and forget about what I was going through.

  Throughout my school career, I have always made good grades, but since the move and everything that was going on,my grades were starting to slip a little bit. Not majorly, but a "C" here or there. Everytime I received a "C" on my report card, I would be grounded from going over to my grandmother's house for six weeks until the next report card came out. That, along with cheerleading and choir kept me motivated to make a "B" and above in all of my classes.

My godmother would reach out to me from time to time, and on one occasion, she even got permission to come and pick me up. She took me to my favorite restaurant, and as we sat to eat, we began talking. We talked about her life, mine, and everything in between. She asked me how was school, how I was feeling; and the most obvious question of all…how did I like being at my uncle's house? I told her, in detail, about everything that was going on and when we returned back to the house, she confronted my uncle's wife and they had a brief disagreement. I never heard my godmother's voice again after that. She often sent me holiday cards with money inside through the mail, but after a while, they started to trickle off.

Now, my grandmother and my grandfather (who died of Lupus before I was born) had a total of five children. Four boys, and my mother was the only girl. One of my uncles, who lived in Las Vegas at the time, flew down to Texas to visit family and friends for the Thanksgiving holiday. As we were all standing around in the kitchen, the kids in the house flocked around him. You know when you have that ONE uncle that all the kids love to be around? Well, he was that one. He began to ask us one-by-one what we wanted to be when we grew up. I remember being so excited about this question, because I always looked forward to growing up and having a wonderful career. It was my turn to say what I wanted to be when I grew up and I said, "I want to be a model." My uncle's wife (the one I lived with), was standing around, and she looked at me dead in my eye and replied to me, "Models are pretty;" insinuating that I was not pretty enough to be a model. That totally crushed my heart and I began to shut down.

That was my last little bit that I could take living with my uncle and his family, so over a span of time, I started asking him if I could go live with my grandmother. The first time I asked him, he said, "No." The second time I asked him, he said, "No." And the third time I asked him, he said, "No." I didn't know what else to do but to get my grandmother involved, and all she told me was, she would continue to pray and ask God to grant him a change of heart. So, I proceeded to keep my grades above a "C" so that I could carry on with going over her house on the weekends.

Shortly before my 13th birthday, my grandmother bought me a Discman. You know, one of those portable CD players that came with earphones and had a radio installed in it? Yeah, well mine was all cute; it was purple and decked out with rhinestones. About three weeks later, she noticed I wasn't carrying it around anymore, so she asked me where it was. I explained to her that the batteries were always low and I never had any new batteries to replace the old ones with. She, then, bought me a battery charger (the one you plug in the wall) so I could charge the batteries and continue to use my portable CD player. I was so excited because I REALLY loved music, and listening to it was like a breath of fresh air. One morning before I went to school, I decided to plug in my charger and recharge my batteries so they would be all ready to go upon my return. When I got home, I ran to my room to get my batteries and the charger was not in the plug socket. So, I ran to ask my uncle's wife where it was, and she told me she had thrown it away. She went on to say she didn't want anything plugged up in the walls if I was not using it.

I was devastated. All I could do is go to my room and cry. That weekend, I told my grandmother what happened to the battery charger and I think she had had enough at this point, as well. She arranged to talk to my uncle; and I don't know what happened, but something changed. I went and asked my uncle for the fourth time if I could go live with my grandmother, and he sat me down so we could talk. He explained to me that my mother's wishes were for me to live with him and his wife and that she personally contacted him to ask if they would legally adopt me. My mother wanted me to live in a two-parent home, and to be raised by a man and his wife, preferably within my family. I said to him, "I know my mom wouldn't want me to be in a place where I was unhappy, and I'm just not happy living here with you and your family." He told me to let him think about it a little longer. A couple of weeks later, I went to him for the fifth time and asked if I could go live with my grandmother, and he answered, yes.

"Yes?" I asked.

He said, "Yes, Toye, you can go live with Branny."

I was so excited and couldn't wait to reach out to her and arrange for the move.

LIVING WITH "BRANNY"

Living with "Branny" was a lot more freeing than it was living with my uncle and his family. It was an adjustment to go from a five-person home to a three-person home (my great-grandfather lived with us, as well). I also had to re-adjust to living with a single parent again. It came with a lot more responsibilities. Branny was, and still is, a hardworking woman. She showed me what it was like to be a "go getter." I watched her run her own snow cone stand, become the director of a daycare, clean houses on Sundays, attend college classes, and renovate her home to open up her own daycare business.

She KEPT me in church, and was the one everyone called on when they were going through something and needed a word of prayer. On Wednesday nights, we were at prayer service, on Friday nights we were at choir rehearsal, and on Saturdays we were at church bright and early for Sabbath school, morning service, and evening service. On Sundays, after she would return from cleaning one of her client's homes, we would have what was considered a "yard day." It included things like, cutting and edging the yard, pulling and picking weeds, planting flowers, sweeping and bagging up leftover grass and putting it neatly on the curb to prepare it for trash day. We normally had roles of who would do what- I would cut, and she would edge; and then, we would do the rest together. It was also known that one Sunday a month, we would visit local nursing homes to sing praise and worship songs and serve food. She was a little old school (I mean, she was my grandmother and all), so every few Sundays, she would pull out the scrub board and we would have to wash our white clothes on it, just so I wouldn't get too used to using the washing machine. HA!

Branny wasn't a "rule enforcer" type of parent; she was more of an advisor. She made any child that she dealt with think REAL hard about the decisions they were making, especially the older they became. Her words and her look had you contemplate your actions. Her advisory was not only for my lifestyle choices, but was also for my grades in school. Now, don't get me wrong…if need be, she would pull out her friend named, "Sam" (her favorite belt), and tackle your fanny if you needed it, but that wasn't hardly my case. Branny's way of parenting made me REALLY understand that I was totally responsible for my own actions, and it created the motivation in me to want to make good decisions, not only because she wanted me to, but because I knew I had to for my OWN best interest.

Now, Branny didn't live in the best of neighborhoods, but she didn't allow it to dictate how you dress, act, or spoke. There was no incorrect English, slouching, smacking, inappropriate dressing, or hanging out with any ol' body permitted in her household. If you were going anywhere with her, you needed to be well-dressed, speaking correct English, and sitting up straight.

Coming from a brand new home in suburbia with my uncle and his family, to moving with Branny in a not-so-good neighborhood was an easy adjustment for me. Mainly because of the love, the expectations, and the attention I was getting, it didn't matter the neighborhood or the environment. Switching schools was more of a difficult task for me, and it took some time getting used to. At my new school, children were more laid back and not as motivated to do well and succeed. I noticed the teachers weren't as nice and sweet, either; I'm sure that was a result of the behavioral issues.

Since accepting me in her home, Branny had extra bills and responsibilities. That was very understandable when you add an extra mouth to feed. As I mentioned earlier, she was already considered a work horse, but she wanted to make sure that all of my needs were taken care of; so she continued to keep her side jobs, as well. I wanted to help take the load off of her as much as I could, so one morning, I asked one of my friends if she and her dad could pick me for school, and they agreed. She wasn't really a close friend, but I was excited to ride and chat with her on the way to school. You know, like girls normally do. Well, that one day turned into six whole months. By the third month, the girl who wasn't a really close friend, proved how much she wasn't one cause she stopped riding with us.

It became only her dad and I. The first couple of days riding with him was weird, because he was pretty old and he seemed more like a grandpa than he did a dad. Every morning, my grandmother would wait with me at our front door until he pulled up in front of the house in his old, brown, Ford pickup truck. One morning, my friend's dad asked if I wanted to stop at the store to get some snacks. In school, snacks were crucial because by days end, I would be so hungry, as most kids were, so I agreed. He gave me twenty dollars and told me to use the whole amount. *Cool!* So, I went inside and came out with chips, sodas, candy bars, and bubble gum. I was so excited to share with the kids at school; and that's exactly what I did.

Everyone was all over me in class, giving me their orders. The next morning, the old man gave me another twenty dollars and I went in the store, but as we drove towards the school he pulled over behind an old church building. I asked what we were doing and he started fondling me all over my body. I asked him to stop, but he kept going. This went on for three months. Every morning, when I arrived at school, I remember being so relieved that the ride was over.

I felt so disgusted, violated, and mentally drained. Thinking back, I can recall sitting in class not being able to focus because I was thinking about my morning rides to school. The kids requesting the snacks was the only thing that kept my spirits high, because, by the end of month one, I started charging for the snacks and making a profit. After three months of riding with this old man, I decided I couldn't help Branny anymore, so I stopped coming to the door when he came and started taking the bus. It's sort of crazy, because she didn't even know that's what I called myself doing-helping her. I felt responsible for my mom's passing and having to go stay with other people, so I wanted to help as much as I could. It cost me a lot.

WHEN FAST FOOD & UNHEALTHY EATING BECAME A PART OF ME

Shortly after getting officially settled in Branny's house and adjusted to my new normal, I got my first job. I was just three months shy of going into my fourteenth birthday. One of my cousin's dad owned a chicken shack inside of a local mall and asked if the both of us (my cousin and I) wanted to work there and help out when we could. Of course, me being who I am, I just couldn't turn it down; so I asked Branny, and she granted me her consent. Now, this wasn't your typical situation because normally, the legal age to work was 16 years old, but because it was somewhat of a relative, we made it work.

Working at the chicken shack was really fun. I would be excited after school to rush home, change clothes, and head to work. It kept me busy, and most importantly, it gave me the confidence I needed in myself. It also taught me the significance of responsibility at an early age. I learned how to work the cash register and dispense money on a regular basis, handle customers and their unsatisfactoriness, season and drop chicken and other foods in the deep fryer, clean and keep the kitchen steadily ready to prepare foods, and I learned how to collaborate and work with other companies to order and deliver foods.

One evening while at work, I was sweeping the floor in preparation for closing and my boss made a statement like, "Whew, you're going to make somebody a good wife one day." Me, being thirteen years old, I looked and smiled and brushed it off my shoulder. Honestly, I thought it was a little flattering, until the comments kept coming. I was a little torn inside because I knew his utterances weren't right, but, yet, I still was excited about working there. I never expressed to Branny what was going on because I wanted to handle it on my own, and I knew I wouldn't have a job if she were to say something.

After about two weeks, the sexual comments had stopped; and I was glad of it. I'm guessing because he had seen how much it disturbed me. One Friday afternoon, my cousin invited me over to her dad's house (my boss) to spend a night, watch movies, and hang out. We thought it would be a great idea to stay up late, wake up the next morning, and go to work together. I agreed to it since everything had ceased, and double checked with Branny to see if it was okay. While we were over there, we played, sang, and had girl talk. We ended the night with watching "The Lion King" on VHS tape, and my cousin fell asleep before it was over. My cousin's dad, who was married, made sure everyone else was asleep in the house and came into the living room to tell me to come talk to him in another bedroom. From there, he locked the door and took my virginity. I didn't want to do it; I looked up to him.

I didn't know what to think of it. I was mad, sad, confused, hurt, and flattered all at the same time. I went home and convinced Branny to buy me a burger and fries, and I pushed what happened WAY in the very back of my mind. I held it inside until I couldn't anymore; so I told my cousin, and she decided to write about it in her diary. When she left her dad's house to move back with her mom, the diary page fell out of the book and the secret had been let out of the bag. His wife found it and called me and Branny up and cursed us both out. I was hurt, confused, and I started to blame myself for what had happened. Even though he was a grown man and he was the one who needed to be cursed out, I felt the blame was placed all on me.

After the sexual abuse incident, the habit of eating unhealthy foods started to creep upon me. I mean, we weren't eating healthy food to begin with, but at least we were eating decent meals that were somewhat healthy. I started to crave foods that we didn't eat on the norm. Things like burgers, fried chicken wings, french fries, pizza, fried foods, etc.; and since Branny was a single, working parent, I was the one cooking those types of foods for our household, or we just simply ate out. Now, because of my genes, my body did not reflect what I ate, but it definitely played a part in who I'd become.

BECOMING A MOM

Before I started dating, I always had the ideal boyfriend/husband in my head that actually became a real list that I prayed over daily. You know, those make believe plans teenage girls have of how they want their future husband and life to be? Yeah, well, that was me. On my list, I wanted him to have a relationship with God, be loving and romantic, work in the corporate world, have an athletic build, and have a tattoo on his left arm (I thought at least one tattoo on a man is sexy). I wanted to have three beautiful children by him, live in a dream home, and live happily ever after. Let's just say he had ALL of these wonderful characteristics and qualities, now, all I needed to do was be that, so I can get that. I didn't know that yet, though.

The "dating rule" at Branny's house was sixteen years old. My cousins (which were my only close friends and approximately the same age as me) all started getting boyfriends and going out on dates when we were halfway through our fifteenth year and I was the only one out of the bunch who was still single. Instead, I would spend my weekends with Branny; and, of course, to a fifteen year old teenager, that was really lame and boring. So, I eventually convinced her to allow me to start dating a little earlier. I remember her yelling, "Alright! Imma turn you a-loose!" in her frustrated voice. Meaning, she was going to let go of that strong hold grip she had on me when it came to dating and men. But, when she "turned me a-loose," she didn't teach or tell me anything about being sexually active, birth control, or protection; because she felt as though, if she taught or told me about it, it would give me permission to do it.

A couple of weeks later, one of my cousins and I went to the movies inside of a local mall, and I met this guy. He and his friends were standing behind us in line and my cousin and I didn't have enough money to get in the movies, so he paid for our tickets. This flattered me, and I thought, *"Wow, that was really sweet. He thought enough of me to buy our tickets."* And, of course, from there the guy and his friends sat with us at the movies; and after it was over, they took us home. Now, this guy didn't have all of the qualities I wanted in a man, but he was cute, he paid for my ticket so he was sweet, and he had a car to take me out on dates.

So, I wanted to get to know him more, and we began talking on the phone and that, eventually, led him to being my boyfriend.

So, because my dad wasn't around growing up, I had what they call, "daddy issues." Issues like, desiring older men and looking for father figures in them, holding on to their every word, and when they fell short, not holding them accountable or leaving, not knowing how a man should love and treat me, and understanding the value I possessed as a young woman. All of these things were not instilled in me during my younger years and my choices in men reflected that. So, I began to be sexually active, trying to fill voids without even noticing.

Shortly after my sixteenth birthday, I missed my period and I found out I was pregnant. I was a sophomore in high school. What was I going to do? What was Branny going to think? How was I going to raise a child? Either way, I knew I needed to break this news to Branny. She came to me one morning before school and told me that God gave to her in a dream that I was pregnant. I lied to her and told her it wasn't true. I felt REALLY bad because I had never lied to my grandmother before. The next morning before I went to school, I wrote a letter and left it in an area in the house where I knew she would find it. In the letter, I told her that I was pregnant and that I was sorry for lying about it to her. When I returned home from school, there was a letter on my bed from Branny. One thing that really stood out to me that she said in the letter was, "A lying mother brings on a lying child." She also told me that I could make it; and she encouraged me to keep going. Well, I took that and ran with it.

While pregnant, I "leveled up" in life quite a bit. I started eating what I thought was healthier for me and my child, I went to tutoring and did extra credit in school, and I got out of the relationship with my boyfriend (the father of my child), who obviously did not want to be in a committed relationship at that time. When I gave birth to my daughter, I remember holding her and looking at her in her precious eyes for the very first time and telling her, "It's just me and you for a while. It's just me and you." At that very moment, I promised myself that I was going to do all I could to give her everything I didn't have growing up.

FINDING MY DAD

One afternoon, I was cleaning up our guest bedroom at home and I found this blue child support card with a name on it. I went to Branny and asked her who's name was on the card and she told me that she thought it was my dad's name. I had no idea that my dad was on child support. So, I did a little investigating. When I was seven months pregnant I took my VERY pregnant self to the courthouse to do some research, and I found more paperwork on my case. From the paperwork, I was able to find out my dad's name and information about my birth and his parental rights. From that paperwork, I concluded that he had signed over his rights when I was nine years old so that my uncle and his wife could legally adopt me. Do you remember me telling you earlier in the story that my uncle's wife had met up with this lady at McDonald's, and they had sent me off to play? Well, come to find out, this lady was my dad's wife. On that day at McDonald's, my dad's wife was meeting with my uncle's wife to sign over their parental rights. I didn't find this out until later, but my dad was married when I was conceived. I have a half sister that is four months older than I am, so that means that both my mom and my dad's wife were pregnant at the same time. This also means, I was "the other woman's child," and that explained why he had nothing to do with me in the first place. I don't recall him being at my mom's funeral, either.

Branny very vaguely remembered who my dad was, but she had an idea about where his aunt stayed. One Sunday afternoon, we went driving around looking for my dad's aunt's house. Of course, she prayed before we left, but after visiting two wrong houses, the third house was a match. I knocked on the door and someone answered, and I asked if they knew my dad. The guy responded, "Yes! That's my uncle." I told him that the man I was looking for was my dad and he invited me in to give me his phone number. The guy then told me a little about my dad and instructed me to give him a call on his day off.

After school one Monday, I came home and decided to give my dad a call. I was nervous and anxious inside. My palms started to sweat and my heart was BEATING out of my chest, or so it felt. He answered the phone and I asked if I could speak to him. I, then, went on to tell him that I was his daughter, and then there was silence. "Hello? Hello?" I said. He then said, "Yeah, I'm here," followed by, "Wow, ok...hey!" I didn't know how he was going to respond to me, so I was brief and short with the conversation and asked him if he would like to meet me in person. I met up with him, and from there, we began trying to mend a broken relationship. I had to forgive him. And, even though I still don't have all of the answers of what happened, I understand that things happened the way they did for a reason.

Toye Penny
CEO MOM LIFE

When I graduated from high school, my daughter was one year old. I was extremely proud of myself. I had worked hard and stayed in school even with the hardships of being a teen mom, and my daughter was present and able to witness me walk across the stage. That was a great accomplishment for me, and I had high hopes and intentions of doing even greater things. After graduating, I was advised to stay close to home because

I needed support with raising my daughter. Though I had many colleges I was looking into, I had no access to child care being far away from home. So, I did what I was advised to do...I stayed close to home. Around this time, I thought I was really grown. I was eighteen years old, I had a baby, a car, was in school working towards a career, had a job at the local mall, and had a little extra income coming in from child support. There was nothing anybody could tell me; I thought I was pretty much grown. Huh. Little did I know…

For the most part, I was a good child; given everything that I had been through, I was rather humble. But, every now and then, I would smart mouth Branny; until one day, she'd had enough. She explained to me that there was only one grown person in the house and if I wanted to be grown, I needed to get out in the world and "be grown." So, that's exactly what I did. I took my daughter, loaded my car with my clothes, and left. I had NO idea where I was going. I tried asking family members if I could live at their place for a while; after all, I had done many of them favors prior to me moving out…but all of their answers were no. Go figure.So, I found myself living out of my car; all because I was being stubborn. The crazy things we do as teenagers, right?

I lived out of my vehicle for a couple of weeks until Branny decided to come and get the car because the insurance was in her name, and it had expired. I thought she was the meanest person in the world. So, I asked a cousin if I could come live with her and her children for a couple of months while I found somewhere to stay, and she welcomed me in. My daughter's grandparents suggested that she come live with them for a couple of months until I found a stable place to be, so that's what I did. While at my cousin's house (she felt more like an aunt), everything was going pretty good as I would wake up, pray, jog, and go to work and come back to do it all over again. I knew this was not the route that I wanted my life to take, so I really tried to keep positive as I was going through this, and come out on top.

Until one day, my child support money came up missing. I was devastated. I needed it, along with my work income, to pay for my school tuition that was coming up. While getting some chicken tenders from a fast food restaurant one day, I met this man who was thirteen years my senior. This man had a couple of things on my "boyfriend/husband list," so we started talking, and eventually dating. I fell deeply in love with him for what I thought was the right reasons, but mainly because he was there in my time of need. When I needed someone to talk to, he was there. When I needed a hug, he was there. When I needed a shoulder to cry on, he was there.

Back at my cousin's house, my money came up missing once more, and another time after that. It got to the point to where I had to sleep with my purse in my arms so it wouldn't come up missing again. I just couldn't take it anymore. I had had enough, so I called Branny to apologize and ask if I could come back home. She agreed as long as I followed the house rules and respected her as an adult of the house. So, I moved back in. By this time, I was truly in love with the older guy that I was dating. But what I didn't know, was that he was in an on again, off again engagement to his long time girlfriend, and they were seeing each other the whole time we were seeing each other.

I was so hurt, but for some reason, I just couldn't let go of him. He was there when I needed him most. That relationship, and all the drama that came with it, lasted for a whole year before I decided I needed to move on and do better things for myself. Now, my heart didn't move that fast, so I kept going back thinking things were going to change, when all the while, he was never the right guy to begin with. Our intentions for being with each other were totally different. I decided to focus on my daughter and I.

While in school to become an RMT (registered massage therapist), I realized that healthy living was something I valued and I wanted to help others live a healthier life, and this was a great start. Shortly after I graduated school and became an RMT, I got hired at a local day spa. I really enjoyed my career. It provided a lot of freedom for my daughter and I, and I was able to move out of Branny's house (on good terms) when I was nineteen, almost twenty years old. I had successfully made it to adulthood, while also being a mother. I worked at the local day spa for four years and the owner really liked me as an employee.

One day, she came to me and asked if I wanted to buy the spa from her because she wanted to go on to do something else. I thought to myself, *"Wow, I knew I wanted to own a business one day, but I didn't know it was going to be this soon."* I thought, for sure, I'd be crazy if I'd passed this up. So, I went home and pondered on it really hard. I was excited, scared, and nervous all at the same time. Afterall, I was just starting to figure this whole "adulting" thing out while trying to juggle motherhood and other responsibilities. I had just gotten a brand new ride, I had an apartment, and so many other things on my plate. After thinking about it long and hard, I decided to say yes to the deal. I just had to get over the hurdle of the money that she wanted.

Of course I didn't have what she asked for up front, so I asked a friend who owned a construction company to attend a meeting with me and help me negotiate with her. Keep in mind, I was twenty-three years old and had no business training, and I had no Idea what I was doing, so I did what I knew. At the time, I had a client that was an attorney, and I was talking to her about it and she asked me if I would like her help. Of course, I didn't turn that down, so we agreed to barter services and she represented me as I closed on the deal to purchase the business. Look at that! I was now a single mother, a day-spa owner, a boss, and a provider all at twenty-three years old. This is when my many roles became real. I was a for real adult now. This is also when things started to get hectic.

Being a woman, who was a single mom and an entrepreneur, was not easy. I was responsible for everything and everyone, and I mean that literally. I had work bills, personal bills, staff, clients, maintenance, supplies, homework, mothering, cooking, cleaning, personal life, relationships, maturing, growth...you name it,

I had it or had to do it. It was sometimes hard to keep up with it, but I managed it all on a broken past and unhealed wounds.

I was boss lady/RMT by day, and mommy by night. I was working so hard trying to juggle all my responsibilities that I forgot about myself and my well-being. I was going so fast that I had no time to deal with all that went on in my life. I was just trying to survive. While maintaining all of these roles, I started snapping at my daughter, having less and less time to spend with her, falling off of my workout routine, eating unhealthy foods, often had headaches, and I started to lose myself in all of the titles. I still maintained a happy spirit, though, because that's just who I was. It also started to hit me that I needed to start dating, because I still had high hopes of one day being married, having more children, and living happily ever after. I forgot I needed to have fun. I forgot to love me.

THE RE-SURFACE OF FAST FOOD & UNHEALTHY EATING

About one year after purchasing the day spa, I built my first house. It was so exciting and fun for my daughter and I. I really wanted to give her all of the things that I didn't have growing up. I was finally building a life for her that I felt that she deserved. Heck, I deserved it, too, after all I had been through. While working as an RMT and running the spa, I knew the importance of eating healthy and taking care of my body, but since life had taken over, I didn't know how to find time to squeeze it all in. It was my utmost desire to walk the life I was encouraging my clients to live, but I just didn't have the time; so I lived half-healthy. At least, I thought I was half-healthy. I decided, multiple times, I wanted to start cooking and eating healthier foods and attend the gym twice a week, but it was a struggle to do that.

As you know, there's a lot to evening time responsibilities as a parent; it doesn't only consist of making meals. On most days, I'd pick up my daughter up from after school care, go to the grocery store, come home to make dinner, help her with her homework, pick out school clothes for the next day, take a bath, eat dinner, and go to bed. There was little to no time for play, as I was really trying to survive it all. Since I'd decided that I wanted to make healthier food choices, cooking dinner began to take even longer because I had to put some thought into it. Two or more hours longer. Yeah well, that didn't last too long. To save on time in the kitchen here's what I started doing instead.... I made Hamburger Helper, chili cheese dogs with chips, ordered pizza, chinese food, fried chicken, fish or went through the drive-through just about EVERY. SINGLE. NIGHT. NO KIDDING!

Cheesy enchilada, beef pasta, and cheeseburger macaroni were my favorite Hamburger Helper flavors to make, and I would create a side dish that included a can of green beans or something close to that. During the day while I was at work, my lunch consisted of fast food and rushed, unhealthy meals, as well. I was constantly making bad food choices, day in and day out. I also found myself craving the same, exact foods I craved when I was thirteen years old and had experienced sexual abuse. Yeah, only this time, it came back with a vengeance. I now had access to buy and pick up my own food, because I was an adult; I had my own transportation and I had my own income. This time around, I started to notice different changes that were not so much the way my body looked, but more so how my body felt; simple, minor, internal changes. They were things like headaches, fatigue, brain fog, constipation, low energy, irritability, and sometimes, mood swings. I simply just blamed it on the stresses of work-life balance; which, I was totally clueless, because I worked out almost everyday, and honestly, I thought that was enough.

One night, after leaving the spa, I found myself feeding my daughter a chili cheese dog and some Doritos for dinner, while I scarfed down four slices of cold pizza that I was too tired to warm up. It was then, I realized there needed to be a shift. Unhealthy leftovers and unbalanced meals could no longer be our story. I immediately searched for a nutrition school and enrolled one month later.

I studied nutrition for one year, and realized that my eating was directly tied to other health areas of my life. By choosing unhealthy foods and going through the drive-thru daily, this was more than just a "I didn't have time" problem. There were deeper issues that needed to be dealt with. My unresolved life matters were manifesting through my eating habits. Then, I had an "Aha" moment. Once I shifted my physical, emotional, and spiritual health, my eating habits would improve, as well. I then began feeling a sense of fulfillment that I had never experienced before.

GOD HEARD MY PRAYERS

By the time I was twenty-seven years old, I had completely made up my mind that I was no longer going to be actively "looking" for a husband. I knew that when my husband arrived, it was going to be because he found me and not the other way around; so I continued to "do me," so to speak. I completely focused on getting to know myself, being a good mom to my daughter, and running a successful business. Everything else was extra and I made time for it when I could. I knew that if I wanted a good husband, I had to be a good wife first (even though I wasn't a wife, yet); and I also believed that you attract who you are, so I definitely wanted to attract a husband with a vibe that matched mine. I dated here and there, but nothing really serious came my way, so I continued on with my life. In my teenage years, I had always told myself that I would model when I became an adult. Modeling was something my mom did, and I wanted to follow in her footsteps, so every modeling opportunity that came up, I would audition, if I had time to spare.

One hot summer, I'd stumbled upon this fashion show that my cousin was attending, and he asked me to audition along with him, so I did. I was selected to be one of the models in the fashion show and it was a great experience. I'd seen this guy and we, sort of, locked eyes, but he looked like he was the man behind the whole show, so I left it at that. The following year, I auditioned for the same fashion show and was selected to be a model once again; and there, I saw this same guy. We locked eyes, as we did the year before, but still nothing happened.

Six months later, the same fashion show was held at the same location, so I opted out of being in the show and Branny and I went to sit, watch, and support my cousin who was one of the models in the show. Again, I saw the same guy and we locked eyes, but this time, he walked up to me after the show and asked for my number to keep in contact. So, I gave it to him. By the following weekend, we went on our first date and I found out that he had mostly everything on my "ideal boyfriend/husband list" that I had been praying over. Even though I wasn't really looking, there was something about him. One thing I did do was, state my intentions and let it be known that I was looking for marriage and to start a family, and if this was something he wasn't looking for, then we weren't going to move any further.

He then told me that his intentions for the relationship were the same as mine. When we gave each other a hug to finalize the date, we both agreed that there was something different about the hug. He told me that I would be his wife one day. In my mind, I was like…"time will tell."

Okay, so listen, there was a twist with this man cause he was from an island AND he had an accent. The U.S. Virgin Islands to be exact, AND he was an ex-militant, a computer geek, AND a vegetarian. OKAY! The Lord heard my prayers, was looking out, and blessed me extra! Since that hug on our first date, we knew it was going to be something different and that this relationship was going to last for a very long time. We ended up dating for three years before he decided to introduce me to his family (I'm guessing he wanted their approval, too). On my 30th birthday, this man surprised me and took me on a trip to the U.S. Virgin Islands to meet his family, and to relax and enjoy a two-week vacation. It was so beautiful. This was a dream come true. Thank you, Lord. I was able to sit back, relax, and enjoy being taken care of for once. This was the perfect getaway.

In order to make this trip possible, I had to rearrange everything back at the day-spa. Staff was not showing up, they were running late, and not handling all of the responsibilities of the business. I eventually had to close the business while I was away, because things weren't being run correctly, which caused me to lose money and not be fully present to enjoy the amazing, beautiful scenery that was in front of me. After visiting three islands and getting a massage on the beach, my mind was clear and I began thinking about how I could be "one" with this man (if he asked me), grow a family, and still keep my business. One of the things I kept in mind was that my daughter was about to become a teenager, and I knew that was going to be a crucial time in her life. I really wanted to be present and give her my undivided attention, while not being so occupied with the stresses of running the day spa, but I knew that I still needed to make a living. So, while soaking in the sun, I prayed and asked God for an answer. How can I go after my dream of being my own boss, get married, have more kids, and still be fully present to raise them?

Our dreamy trip was over and I had a wonderful time, but it was time to get back to reality. On the plane ride back, I was relaxed and super comfy in my chair, and I was thinking about getting back to my daughter and figuring out my current situation. And then, a voice whispered in my ear, "Sell the business."

"What?" I said to myself.

And the voice said it again, "Sell the business."

"No, I can't do that!" I said.

I have been there for such a long time. I started there when I was nineteen. But, God was giving me the answer I had prayed for and instructed me to sell the business. I kept thinking to myself, *"Man! That's Crazy, I'm not doing that!"* So I leaned over to the chair next to me and told my Carribean sunshine.

He said, "Really? If that's what you feel is right." I thought long and hard the whole ride back.

When I arrived home, I started researching and found a commercial broker nearby. I gave him a call, we arranged a meeting, and before I knew it, we started working together. I couldn't believe it. Two weeks later, he found a lovely couple who wanted to start the new year with a business. I interviewed them, they interviewed me, and it was a perfect fit! Two months later, we closed on the deal at a local title company, and I was able to walk away from the day spa with a profit, after seven years of owning it. I could now live out my dreams, watch my daughter grow, start a new business, get married and have more kids. Look at God.

Eight months after the sale of the day spa, I became a fiance! We planned a beautiful wedding for one year later, and we decided that we wanted to start a family right away. We conceived a baby girl one month after our wedding day, and the rest was history. While pregnant, I decided that as a Holistic Health Strategist, I wanted to help moms who were leaders in their industries live a healthier lifestyle, because I thought that if I struggled with it, I knew others did, too. While I was growing my new practice, after being married for three years, we decided we wanted another child and that's exactly what we got. We conceived another baby girl. Now, I am a fulfilled woman, a mom to three daughters, a wife and advocate for career moms, and I couldn't be happier. After the death of my mom, moving from home to home, and all of the other ups and downs that life brought me, things still managed to turn around and work out in my favor.

What It Means To Love You MORE....

"When you become a mom, life becomes even more about you."

Being a mom means schedule changes, erratic nights, shifted priorities, and positioning your decisions around this tiny human being that has entered your world. They eventually grow up, start to hold conversations with you, and have extracurricular activities. Now, you aren't just physically drained, you are mentally and emotionally drained, too. From late night feedings, chasing monsters away, potty training, carpooling to band practice, teacher meetings, homework, after hours school projects, cooking meals, doing laundry, cleaning, teaching, nurturing, chaperoning, disciplining, and so much more, you are barely hanging on by the end of the day. And, if you're married, you must schedule in some time for that, too, because you don't want your marriage to end in the "D-word." So, after the kiddos finally go to bed, you nurture that aspect of your life, too. What about your relationships with your friends, family, and co-workers? Are they tugging for your time, too? You, somehow, balance everyone of these roles, all while successfully managing a career.

When I got pregnant with my oldest daughter and people started to slowly find out about it, a lot of them told me that my life was basically over. They told me that it wasn't about me anymore, that life was all about my brand new bundle of joy that was coming. And yes, while they were right to an extent, my life was definitely altered. I somewhat believed what the majority said and I did exactly what they told me for the first few years of my daughter being on this earth. But, after being a mom for fifteen years, it finally came to me, that things were all backwards.

When you become a mom, life becomes even more about you. I know you are probably thinking, *"Wait, what? This girl is absolutely insane."* But, hear me out for a second. The moment you become pregnant, your body is no longer yours. You are using your mind, body, and spirit to grow a whole human being. Before you became a wife, mom, boss and everything else you juggle, you were a woman, first. You have had issues, insecurities, doubts, and unhealthy habits that probably weren't completely resolved when you became a mom. Whatever unresolved, unhealthy habits or issues you had before you became pregnant will manifest through the growth of your child, and then, eventually, pass on through your parenting. Let's skip to life outside of being a mom...Whatever unresolved, unhealthy habits or issues you had before you got married, will manifest in your marriage. Whatever unresolved, unhealthy habits or issues you had before you acquired that new friend, will show up in your friendship, and so on and so on.

Raising a family while being a top earner can be stressful. Period. It's definitely not for the faint at heart. The reality is... some days the office, spouse, kids, everybody, and everything will get on your last nerve. But, that's not a reflection of them, that's a reflection of your inability to respond or react to them. If there are days that everything is getting on your nerves, it has nothing to do with them and everything to do with how you are pouring into yourself.

Loving you MORE is intentionally making you a priority...mentally, spiritually, physically, emotionally, and nutritionally, so that you can live a lifestyle full of more energy, less stress and create a RIPPLE effect of health and wellness for generations to come.

Today's society defines self-care or "loving yourself" by activities. Things like taking a candle lit bubble bath, watching television, getting a deep tissue massage, and buying your favorite pair of Louboutin red bottom pumps are all defined as self-care. But, when you look at just the activities of self-love, it can seem indulgent, and if you continue to look at self-love as just activities, then it'll always seem that way.

Yet, TRUE self-love is never indulgent. It's necessary. So when you love you more, it's necessary to serve "them." We can't embody success when our bodies are failing.

By continuing to put others' needs before your own, you can not be present for your spouse, kids, work or anything/anybody else. You see, it's often easier for us to love "them," but not put enough emphasis on loving ourselves; when, in fact, that is the ONLY way we can properly love them. If you're serving from an unhealthy lifestyle, what do you think they will receive? This is why our health and other areas of our life fail. All. Because. We. Care.

These are the exact words I had to say to myself the moment I decided that my next level was going to require more. "We are bad stewards over our lives if we continuously do the things that will potentially take us away from our family and society." This means, we may mother well e.g.cook for them, teach them, be good wives, play a good role in society, but if we are not setting an example and not making ourselves a priority we are bad stewards. We all want to be great mothers, but being a great mom means being a great woman first.

> "Take care of the woman in you first so you can take care of 'them' effectively. When you love yourself MORE, the reflection shows in them, through you."

Loving yourself MORE is not about being selfish, self-centered or egotistical; neither is it being perfect, arrogant, or vain. It's about taking care of your every need, first, so that you can effectively take care of "them" (your hubby, kids, family, and society).

HOW TO LOVE YOU MORE...

In my many years of being a mom while running a business, I've tried to figure out a solution on how to balance it all. With the experience of being both a single mom and a married mom with more kiddos and more responsibilities, I have found that loving yourself MORE is not a wish, but it is ESSENTIAL to being a CEO while raising a family.

You are a leader. If you are a mom, you are a leader. If you are a CEO, you are a leader. If you are a wife, you are a co-leader, which is still a leader. Therefore, there is no way you can be a great leader if you are not properly equipped to lead. You must first acknowledge that your needs need to be a part of your schedule.

A question that I often get asked is, "How do you juggle being a CEO and still be a great mom, wife and other things?" Is there a method? Here's what I have to say about that, after spending many years of living the "unbalanced life," I choose to love myself MORE, which has not always been easy. I mean, don't get me wrong, it can be the hardest thing to do when your mindset is stuck on thinking you're being selfish, but once you shift your thinking, it's the most rewarding gift you can give to yourself, your family and your work. There is no truth to real balance. I mean, let's think about this, MomFriend... you are juggling kids, laundry, meals, marriage, work duties, employees, relationships, etc. Life happens! And, with kiddos, everyday is unpredictable. No matter how many routines you have in place, something always happens to throw you off your schedule.

You can not be everywhere at the same time. You just can't. No matter how much you think you can, if you focus on one particular thing, something else will always go lacking. What balance is for one mom, may not be your same balance. You have to purposely search and find what works for you. And no, it's not an easy task, but let me tell ya, it can be very much so accomplished.

Here's what I've also found to be true…be FULLY present wherever you are, in whatever you're doing. If you're at work, be fully present. With your self care, be fully present. If you're spending time with the kiddos or the hubby, or anyone else…Be. Fully. Present. When you are fully present, you are giving your undivided attention to whatever task you have at hand and you are saying to them, or it, *"I am all in at this present moment;"* and then work hard at it and do it. If you're with hubby, don't talk about the kiddos because you won't be fully present and he will feel that. You owe that to him and your marriage. After all, it's the love that you all had for each other that created the kiddos in the first place. If you are with the kiddos, don't be on your phone focused on work, be fully present. They will appreciate the undivided time and attention you are giving them. The one thing that will give you true "mom guilt" is when your kids tell you you're always on your phone or computer and you never pay attention to them. Believe me, I've heard it all before. You don't want them searching for love in all the wrong places; they need it from you first. This is why making yourself a priority will help you find your balance. And don't forget to give yourself grace to mess up and drop the ball. You are a woman, and even though you have plenty of superpowers, knowing it all is not one of them.

MOMFRIEND! IT'S TIME WE START SHOWING UP FOR OURSELVES!

CEO Moms have the ability to run WILDLY successful businesses. We are the greatest caretakers but are notorious for neglecting our own needs. We put ourselves after work, kids, spouses, siblings, parents, friends, co-workers, neighbors and even our fur babies.

STATISTICS BRAIN reports that "86% of CEO moms say they frequently feel stressed," AMERICAN PSYCHOLOGICAL ASSOCIATION says "49% of CEO moms say their stress has increased over the last 5 years."

31% of moms reported eating as a way of managing stress with overeating and/or eating unhealthy foods and only 35% of moms reported exercising once a week or less, citing fatigue and time as the main reason.

> But What We Fail To Realize Is... In Order To Sustain & Properly Serve Others... We Must First Serve Ourselves

When you stand up and show up for yourself everything and everyone else falls into place. You are the most important ingredient in this recipe.

> *It is impossible to say "I love me," but deny yourself the ability to care or prioritize yourself.*

YOU HAVE ALREADY ACCOMPLISHED SO MANY THINGS, BUT YOUR NEXT LEVEL IS GOING TO REQUIRE MORE!

In order to be TRULY healthy and love you MORE, you must do the work on yourself. The way I see things, we should pay attention and treat the body, mind, spirit and soul as a whole. In other words, holistically. When you take care of EVERY aspect of your life, that my friend, is Living. A. Healthy. Lifestyle.

One thing that literally "BLOWS MY BUBBLE" is when I hear people say, "I need to live a healthy lifestyle," but they don't treat ALL aspects of their body. They simply just try to exercise more and eat what they call "healthy," but they continue to carry around so much stress, or take pills on a regular basis just to get sleep at night. This is what most people think living a healthy lifestyle is. I mean, don't get me wrong, eating "healthy" and exercise is great, but if you are doing those things and still not taking care of the other areas of your life, what's the point?

I created what I call "The Love You More Method™," it's an eight step method to help you make yourself a priority and adapt a healthier lifestyle without going CRAZY in the process, because as we know, trying to live a healthier lifestyle can sometimes make you feel a lil coo-coo. As I stated before, there are eight total elements that you need to have more energy, feel more balanced and be that leader you were meant to be. The first seven are primary.

These elements are:

1. A meaningful spiritual practice.
2. Never ending self-maintenance.
3. Empowering physical activities.
4. Relationships that nurture your soul.
5. Quality sleep.
6. Mental and emotional peace.
7. A thriving career.

I like to refer to the first seven as *PRIMARY FOODS*. Primary foods feed you, but they don't come on your plate.

The very last element of a healthy lifestyle is:

8. Foods that nourish you and your body.

THIS ELEMENT IS SECONDARY. SECONDARY FOODS are foods that actually come on your plate. They are healthy, align with you and your body, and are nourishing at the same time. These foods are just a secondary source of energy.

The more primary food we receive, the less we depend upon secondary foods. The opposite is also true. The more we fill ourselves with secondary foods, the less we are able to receive the primary foods of life. Take a moment to ponder on that…

For example, we all know a mom friend (maybe it's you) who has the perfect diet, but her life is dramatic, full of hurt and pain, and all over the place. Or maybe on your path to having a healthy lifestyle, you work out quite a bit, but late night thoughts in your head cause you to sleep, but not be fully rested and you end up groggy and easily irritated, have low self-esteem, hurt, or to be mean and bitter. Or maybe you have a happy, healthy lifestyle, but the foods you're eating are contributing to depression and low energy levels.

My mom was thirty-one years old when she died. I came to the conclusion that all of the pieces to the puzzle were not together in her life, either. How could it be when she was a young woman and still learning? Just like the majority of us, she fell short in her primary and secondary areas of her life. She did the best she could with what she knew, and that makes her no different from you and I. There was no one that taught her about the primary and secondary foods of life and how to love herself more so she can properly nourish others. They didn't know, either.

When "love myself first" came to mind… I was sitting alone in my car thinking, and I asked myself out loud, "How can I love me MORE when I've gone through so much pain, rejection, and hurt in my life? How can I love me MORE when others didn't?" The truth is, I started to follow the eight simple elements of a healthy lifestyle that I mentioned above, and things started to shift for me. I began feeling a sense of fulfillment that I had never experienced.

Even though I had gone through all of the heartbreak and disappointments, I am now properly equipped to handle them and deal with other things life throws my way. I came to realize that without the twists and turns of life, I wouldn't be the woman I am today. As a matter of fact, I wouldn't be writing this book for you to read. Each event that took place in my life served a purpose, and has prepared me for what's to come. I am just more equipped this time around.

Maybe you've experienced a death, rejection, divorce, rape, sexual, physical or emotional abuse, miscarriage, or some other horrific incident in your life, and it has caused your secondary foods to be off balance. Or maybe your life is filled with hugs, love, healthy relationships and everything that is primary, but you can't understand why you are still feeling down. Or, just maybe, your life is filled with kale, quinoa, and vibrant salads, but you don't understand why your energy levels are low and you have constant headaches with frequent mood swings and everything someone says to you, it ends with a snap.

Whatever your case is, having a healthy lifestyle is not ONLY about eating healthy and working out. It's. So. Much. More. It's about being healthy, whole and complete within yourself, finding the root of your problems and living a life that's truly happy and healthy so you can better serve and support others. When you align your primary and your secondary foods by following the eight elements of a healthy lifestyle, life for you, too, will begin to shift towards health, energy, happiness, and fulfillment. When you start living a healthier lifestyle, it will not only benefit you, but it will benefit "them," too.

By using these 8 elements you will develop healthy LIFESTYLE skills that will help you go from...

- A Meaningless Religious Routine To Meaningful & Fulfilling Spiritual Practice
- Exhausted & Drained To Prioritized Daily Self Care
- Average, Unaligned Workouts To Empowering Physical Activities
- Transactional Relationships To Nurturing & Reciprocal Connections
- Overworked & Compromised Sleep To Well Rested & Full of Energy
- Disturbed & Off Balance To Mental & Emotional Peace
- Guilty & Dissatisfied To A Thriving Professional Life
- Unhealthy Food Choices To The Intentional Consumption of Healthy Foods

Primary Foods...

Since primary foods are our primary source of energy and feed us, but don't come on our plate, let's focus on these elements first. Then, the secondary will follow.

ELEMENT #1/A MEANINGFUL, SPIRITUAL PRACTICE
Internal Spiritual Fuel

How many times have you recognized that you were off balance spiritually, but had no time to correct it because you were overwhelmed with work, family & other responsibilities?

You know, in my first business, I was really torn on whether to share the love of God to others. I was young and still trying to figure things out; and even though I had a growing relationship with Him, I wasn't too sure if my workplace was the right environment for me to share, so I kept quiet. Ohhhh, but now! I have grown; and I have been through too many things to not share the goodness of God. As a matter of fact, the ONLY thing that has kept me through life's turmoil was God himself. From my story that you read in the beginning of this book, I could've turned out differently, or ended up somewhere else. But, He faithfully and continuously sees me through and gives me strength to make it throughout my days, even when I don't deserve it.

Now, I'm not trying to push my faith on you, whatever your spiritual practice is, I want you to focus on that. However, I do want you to understand that this element is about moving from a Meaningless Religious Routine To Meaningful & Fulfilling Spiritual Practice. This element plays a huge role in your peace and sanity. For me, a spiritual practice is everything. It gives me life, hope, courage, peace, joy and so much more. To give honor, respect, and thanks to God who thought of me enough to create me with my own individual fingerprint that no one else in this world has, is so important to me. For that, I'm grateful.

With that being said, in order to maintain a healthy lifestyle as a leader, nourishing your soul is just as important as nourishing your body. I mean think about it, before you were blessed with a physical body, you were blessed with a soul. Take the time to honor it. You must feed it and replenish it to get you through your tough times in life. Listen, there's an old saying… "Whatever is in your spirit will come out;" and when I tell you that is so true!! If you're angry, sad, and depressed, it will reflect in the words that you speak and the actions that you take. Just the same as if you are happy, joyful, and peaceful.

When you've just walked in the house, boggled down with grocery bags, the baby is crying, your boobies are engorged and leaking, you're tired and just want to sit down and call it a day, is your spirit filled with what it takes to handle your two year old's tantrum? When you've completed a long day of work after your most reliable employee didn't come through like she always does, now it's time to go home to deal with the kiddos, and hubby just came home and said he needs some quality "one-on-one time," do you have the spiritual reserves to deliver what's needed from you? When you've heard your teenager snap one too many times, and you want to snap right back upside their head, do you have the grace not to do so?

> 2 Corinthians 12:9 says... "And he said unto me, My grace is sufficient for thee: for my strength is made perfect in weakness. Most gladly therefore will I rather glory in my infirmities, that the power of Christ may rest upon me."

Which means, God has enough grace for you, even in your imperfections. As a matter of fact, his power is stronger when you're weak. So, it's absolutely okay to acknowledge and say out loud when you feel defeated, because that's when you will find strength in Him, and His power will work *in* you *through* Him.

By feeding your soul and trusting God more, you are filling yourself up so that you can adequately pour out to "them." There is ABSOLUTELY NO WAY you can give to someone else and you don't have it for yourself. Period. Having a spiritual practice and trusting God more does not mean you are perfect and life won't happen to you. As a matter of fact, life will happen to you MORE, but as you replenish with Him, you will have an overflow to give to yourself and others.

Now, I'm not going to lie, trusting God COMPLETELY is a daily struggle (even for me), because as women, in the twenty-first century, we work hard and pride ourselves in handling it all and it can seem difficult to relinquish things completely to someone we can't physically see. I get it! But, we can't handle our part and His part, too! We have to remember to not only do what we can as moms, wives, leaders, motivators, educators and so much more, but to give Him complete control of the things that we can't see happening right now.

Don't just touch on creating a spiritual practice, focus on creating a meaningful and maintainable spiritual practice. It doesn't matter how others justify their connection with God, this is about you re-establishing and prioritizing your connection to your source so that you can be everything that you need to be and more and positively spill over to others that you come in contact with.

Here are a few ways you can go from a meaningless religious routine to a meaningful and fulfilling spiritual practice:

WHEN YOU WAKE UP

Take the time to honor and show gratitude for the day and the breath that was provided for you. Most of us don't wake up begging for air to breathe, it's provided for us naturally. Take a moment and embrace your air. Make it a point to get up early before anyone in the house and read a devotional scripture/inspirational quote and pray/meditate. If you co-sleep and it's hard to sneak out of bed without waking anyone, lay in the bed and say, "Lord, thank you." Whichever one you choose, a prayer or scripture, that will be what you meditate on throughout your day. For example, if your devotional is Philippians 4:13, *"I can do all things through Christ who strengthens me,"* when you face struggles at the office, go back to that scripture. At home, when the kiddos are acting up, go back to that scripture. When the hubby's got an attitude...Go. Back. To. That. Scripture.

When You Are Getting Ready

If you find it difficult to get up and read a scripture and pray first thing in the morning because of your hectic schedule or the kiddos won't let you have a lil "me" time, put on a YouTube sermon of your favorite pastor or motivational speaker and listen to the word. What you hear, see, say, and read all contributes to how you will respond to your day. When my kiddos constantly interrupt me during my daily devotional, I grab my phone, turn on Bishop T.D. Jakes, turn on my curling irons and GET TA CURLING! All while listening, hearing, and absorbing the word, curling my hair, and looking after my baby girls. I also love to put my favorite scriptures on a sticky note and stick them on my bathroom mirror so I can see them while I'm getting dressed.

While You're Riding In The Car

Ok, I don't know about you, but my vehicle is like a breath of fresh air when I hop in. You always have a place to talk on the phone, think, and sing without any disturbances. When I put my music on, I get in my zone. Don't let it be a nice day outside, 'cause the windows are coming down and the sunroof is poppin' open. It's super easy to get yo' praise and worship on in the car; you can either turn on some music, or again, turn on the word. Not only that, sit in silence and say, "Lord, I thank you" over and over again, and watch those tears of gratefulness start rolling.

Love "THEM," Love YOU More

Throughout Your Day

When you arrive at work, recognize that it is a gift to be able to do what you love. Girl, it's a gift to even have a career. So many people are struggling without work and you have exactly that, plus it's what you love doing... show gratitude towards it. If it's something that you are not happy with, say, "Thank you, Lord, for my work that you created me to do. I know you have something greater for me, but until you bless me to get there, thank you anyhow." Don't just get to work and turn on your "work-slay mind." Constantly remind yourself who God has called you to be, thank Him, and live it. When you are picking up the kiddos, thank Him for your children and pray over them, when you are cooking dinner, glorify His name. Even when you see your hubby walk through the door, thank God for him and give him a hug and secretly pray over him (even if he gets on your last nerve). Also, remember to serve others and give where you are lead. There are several ways to involve God throughout your day, find one or several that you love and stick to it.

At The End Of The Day

When everyone is finally asleep and you lay your head down to rest for the night, make it a point of spending a moment to thank Him and ask for peace throughout the night while you and your family sleep. Be grateful for your day and what tomorrow holds. Whatever happened that put you into worry mode, know that you did all you could, trust His will and go to bed. And, please don't tell me that I'm the only MomFriend who sometimes be so tired that as soon as I lay down and say my prayer, my eyes close and I fall asleep during the whole thing and wake up like, "Where was I, Lord?" HA! No, but He knows your heart and will honour that.

> Take a moment and jot down some ways below that you plan on including and glorifying God in your daily activities...

_____

_____

_____

_____

_____

_____

_____

_____

_____

_____

_____

ELEMENT #2/NEVER ENDING SELF-MAINTENANCE
Internal Physical Fuel

Self care provides the attention that you deserve to perform each day. While it is not uncommon for people like us to pick up a routine of self care, it's more unlikely that we maintain those habits. Between balancing personal, family, business, spiritual, physical/nutrition, and so much more, it is important that no matter what is on the agenda that we stay the top priority.

So, what exactly is self-care? What does it mean to you? Is it getting your hair done once a month? Is it going for a jog? Or is it something deeper than that? Before becoming a Holistic Health Strategist, what came to mind for me was something physical, and it took place every couple of weeks, and definitely, not daily. When I was thirteen years old and first moved with my grandmother, she introduced me to my beautician. I would visit her salon once a month, and when I became an adult, my visits increased to every two weeks. Now that I have more kiddos and life is a little bit more hectic, I'm back to once a month, again. Believe it or not, till this day, that same lady still does my hair. Hey, Pam!

If you google the definition of self-care it reads: "The practice of taking an active role in protecting one's own well-being and happiness, in particular, during periods of stress."

My definition of self-care is: "The necessary application of serving your mind, body, spirit, soul and nutrition on a

> *DAILY basis so you can feel more energized, joyous and fulfilled to do the work you were called to do and better serve others."*

You see MomFriend, self-care is not a one time thing. It's continuous. It's a constant repetition of tiny habits that ensure that you are the best you. It's not only limited to your outer appearance either. When you serve yourself DAILY...mind, body and spirit...and not only during periods of stress, you are making a conscious decision to respect and love yourself MORE. When that decision is made by you and only you, your kiddos and everyone else (including the family dog) will do so, as well. Let's think about it for a second, the most important person in a restaurant is the chef. Without the chef, there's no lavish meals. The most important person in a classroom is the teacher. Without the teacher, there will be no lesson. The most important person in a household with kiddos, are the parents. Without you, your children would be lost. And although they may find their way later in life (as I did), it would still show up, in some way, that you were not present.

NOW LISTEN UP! Some people (including your kiddos, hubby, and family members) may not understand, may not like it, and think it's selfish that you serve yourself daily. They may not like the fact that you are filled with joy and taking time away from their needs to fulfill yours. You will probably hear, "Are you doing that, again?"... "I've got cheerleading practice"..."Why are you always doing things for yourself?"... "You're so selfish"...

"Don't go, Mommy. I need you here with me." This is when the guilt starts to come in. Motherhood is not pretty all of the time, especially when combined with a career. Remember, it's not for them to understand at this moment. You are a caregiver, nurturer, and one of the leaders of the household (if not the leader); you must set an example for everyone else, no matter how difficult it may be. One day your kiddos will have children of their own and they will then understand the example and the impact you had in their lives.

Set boundaries, and let them know that when you have a red sign on the door, you will be doing yoga, reading or whatever you may be doing. When you remove it, that's when your special self-care time is up. If possible, start this practice when your kiddos are young so as they get older, they will know that self-care is something you value.

By making self care never ending, you will be equipped with the daily renewable fuel that it is so that you are always in a space to perform and respond to your life demands with more energy and abundance.

If you are not serving yourself daily through self-care, don't get all messed up and start having mama drama.

Here are a few simple ways you can start caring for yourself DAILY…

Eat Nourishing Foods

Eating foods that nourish you and your body is one of the BEST things you can do for yourself (see secondary foods section for more in depth details on this subject). It not only gives you the energy you need to sustain your busy days, but it becomes who you are…

your thoughts, your blood, your skin, your mood, etc. I do want you to remember that no one diet works for everyone, so choose the foods that give you the energy and nourishment that you need.

Date Yourself

There's nothing like a good ole date day/night with you. When you date yourself, you'll become more aware of what you like and who you are outside of mom, wife, CEO, and the rest of the roles you juggle. When you know who you are and what you like,

you will then know what you are not, and others will treat you accordingly. Maybe you like going to the movies, doing yoga, sitting and reading a book, roller skating, hiking, singing lessons, drawing, attending a cooking or dance class, going to a restaurant or maybe even going to a play. Sometimes, dating yourself even means locking yourself in your room and watching your favorite television shows for a couple of hours. Whatever it means to you, spend an hour (or two, if you can) alone doing something that brings you joy. If going out in public by yourself feels weird at first, start with something small, like sipping green tea at a small café. Remember, this whole experience is about you learning to love yourself a little more than usual. Period. Don't start overthinking about what people may think because you are alone. It's not about them, it's about your well-being. Heck, you may even meet a new friend; some people like to approach others when they are sitting alone. If that's the case, get their contact info and send them on their way. We don't want them intruding on your time. Whatever your dream date day/night is, start brainstorming some ways of how you can make that happen and act upon it.

Quiet-Time

When you are a mom (especially one with a career), you are highly sought after and needed. There are not many moments that are just pure quiet. From little kiddos to big kiddos, the dog, cat, hubby, clients, co-workers, cell phone, I mean SOMEONE is going to disturb your quietness. And that's perfectly fine, as long as you reserve a time for mental silence. Quiet time is a time set aside in a certain place where you can be alone and draw nearer to God or yourself. This is a proven tactic to help the brain perform better. When having quiet time, first decide on what activities you will be doing. Will you be having bible study, reading, praying, meditating or sitting in silence? Or, maybe even alternating between several different things? After you decide what you will be doing, then you will need to decide on a time. If you use an electronic calendar, as I do, put it on repeat so it will pop up daily on your phone; and when the reminder goes off, get to it! Remember the key is consistency so that this can become a lifestyle. Start with a small amount of time, like ten minutes, and then gradually move up as you see fit. After time, you'll want to decide on a place. Will this place be your closet, office, or the laundry room? Since this is quiet time, you want to choose a place free from distractions and comfortable for you to let your guard down. If you find it hard to locate a place that is free from distractions, then your second choice would be to have "loud-time." Loud time is when everyone around you is going about their normal routine, and you zone out for a bit to draw nearer to God or yourself (come on Mom Friend, let me know I'm not the only one who does this). I've found that when I'm in the midst of my day (at work or at home), revelations can sometimes come to me more often than when I'm sitting in the quiet. If this is you, too, when your calendar goes off and you are not able to sit in quietness alone, stop whatever you're doing and get your ten minutes of loud-time in. Quote your favorite scripture and meditate on it, say a quick prayer, or compliment yourself and focus on that compliment. Sometimes, your best encouraging moments can come in the loud.

Sexy Up Your Wardrobe

Listen...Yes! Moms with careers can live a healthy lifestyle, love the Lord, wife her hubby, be sexy, and raise good humans all at the same time.

Just because you're a mom with a career doesn't mean your sexiness has to completely dissipate. In fact, this gives you even more of a reason to take your sex appeal to a WHOLE NOTHA LEVEL! Think about it, we exude all of this external sexiness before we get married and have kiddos, and then, BOOM! Nothing! We get so occupied with becoming a mom and taking care of everything and everyone else that it, sort of, just falls by the wayside. I get that you're tired, you have long days, and sometimes even longer nights, I get that some days you don't even have the energy to get out of bed, and I even get that you don't feel sexy after having to juggle so much mentally, physically, and emotionally. But, Mom Friend, hear me out for a second! If you're confident internally, sexy will show, externally. Maybe you've never felt confident or sexy inside, or maybe you did at some point and you lost it. But, while you and I are currently working on the internal aspects of a healthy lifestyle, let's talk about the external aspects for a bit. There's one sure way to divvy up your confidence, and that is to sexy up your wardrobe. Now, by adding a little sexiness to your wardrobe, I don't mean wear less clothing, more make-up, lots of hair spray, and a gazillion accessories. I mean, adding little details to your wardrobe that will make you feel sexy inside. Because, remember, if you feel sexy inside, it will reflect in your walk, your talk, and how you show up for yourself, your family and the public. How you dress, whether it's a blazer paired with a skirt or some sweats and a baseball cap, doesn't always have to be for someone else. It's for you, first, and whoever sees it will benefit from it. Stop making it about "them" and more about you. Ok, enough about why you need to sexy up your wardrobe, let's get into what that looks like for you. There are many ways to do this but here are a few:

GET SEXIER BRAS AND PANTIES:
Wearing sexy bras and panties doesn't have to always be for a special occasion. Go to your favorite panty shop (we all know it will most likely be Victoria's Secret) and choose at least six pairs of new, sexy panties and two sexy bras. You want to start small so you don't get overwhelmed, and then work your way up as you get more in the habit of buying sexy. Choose a day-time panty, a night-time panty, a day-time bra, and a night-time bra that's sexy to you (don't go granny on me here). Get three of each, totaling six pairs of panties, and one of each, totaling two, for the bras (Make sure your bras fit you comfortably and are not digging into your skin and adding tension to your neck and shoulders, as this will definitely ruin your mood and take away from your feeling of confidence and sexiness). Your day-time panties and bras will be different from your night-time panties and bras, because they are more of a dressy-sexy caliber than your night-time, which will be more of a casual-sexy. Personally, I have three panty drawers…one dedicated to day-time panties, one dedicated to night-time panties, and one dedicated to cycle-time panties. However you decide you want to organize your panty drawer is definitely your decision, but having sexier under garments is a great way for you to start feeling more confident and sexy, and no one will even know why. It will be your little secret.

WEAR GIRLY NIGHTIES:
Remember before you got married and had kiddos, you went to bed in those cute little night shirts or matching tops with the cute shorts; or was that just me? Girl, I would wash my make-up off, have time to put my face mask on nice and neat, pin my hair up cute and put on lip gloss all before I went to bed. Now, with two more little ones running around, WHO HAS TIME FOR THAT? I'm

doing good if I get a bath, and REALLY good if I have time for a face mask (and it won't be neat)! Believe me, I get it! But, just like your bras and panties, you don't need a special occasion to wear a cute nighty or feel sexy when you go to bed. Choose one of your favorite places that you buy clothes from and start simple. Find at least one matching night set, it could be something satin, cotton, or spandex, whatever is comfortable to you; but, choose a day of the week and wear it. Watch how you feel opposed to putting on an old t-shirt you received from a 5-k run gift bag.

SLAP ON A PAIR OF HEELS:

I don't know about you, but heels always make me feel a little more sexier. It's something about the elevation of your feet paired with a really cute dress or skirt. With heels it's like you have to turn it up a notch because you have to balance, walk gracefully, and command the room when you walk in. Not saying that you shouldn't command the room when you wear flats or tennis shoes (because you most definitely should, that's where your inner confidence comes in), I'm saying there is a different command when a woman walks in with heels on. If you wear tennis shoes or flats more often than heels, that's perfectly fine…do what feels good to you. Spice things up a bit with a pair of your favorite heels, or go buy a pair that you could see yourself wearing. If you don't like wearing heels, that's perfectly fine, too; meet halfway and get a pair of wedge tennis shoes.

These are just a few suggestions of how you can sexy-up your wardrobe, but I would like for you to look deeper into this tip and come up with some new ways (that you don't normally do) and experiment with what you came up with.

Staying On Top Of Your Regular Checkups

This may not sound like your typical spa day, but staying on top of your regular wellness checks are super important. Most check ups are annually, including, womanly exams, breast exams, dental appointments, HPV tests, blood tests, diabetes test, STD test, etc. The more you stay on top of your check ups, the earlier you will be able to detect if anything is an issue. Too many women put off doctor check ups for themselves because they don't have time, or they simply forget. But, hubby's check up is made, kids' appointments are made, and you skip yourself? NO.

As a mom...career or no career, insurance or no insurance, you need to make your check ups a priority. The first step is to make your mind up that you are going to put your needs first. The second step is to call and schedule your appointments. Schedule them with enough time that you can make arrangements for the kiddos, if need be. The third step is to put them on your calendar with at least four reminders to pop up. The reminder should sound off at least one week before, one day before, one hour before, and then, thirty minutes before. The last step is to go. Do not cancel, just go. When you stay on top of your checkups, you stay on top of your life.

Spa Treatments

Coming from being a previous day spa owner, let me tell ya, Mom Friend...there's nothing more luxurious and relaxing than getting away and going to a day spa. Whether you go to one close to home, in a hotel, or have someone come to you, the benefits of the services are phenomenal and you feel great afterwards.

There are several services you can get in a spa, including massages, reflexology, manicures, pedicures, facials, colon hydrotherapy, waxes, hot scrubs, trigger point therapy, cryotherapy, sauna services, the possibilities are totally endless. Finding a good massage therapist, reflexologist, or esthetician can sometimes be a difficult task, but when you do, stick with them if you can. Ask around to see if someone recommends the spa-worker's services, and then use your own judgement to determine if you would like to be a return client or not. Depending on the massage pressure you like, you can definitely ease tension and relax from a great therapeutic massage. I will say, if you are getting reflexology (work that's done on your feet or hands) or massage therapy, you get the best results if it hurts. I know that sounds really crazy, but it's so true. Keep in mind, if your visit is to relax, that's one thing, but if your visit is due to pain, that's another story.

If you are pressed for time and can't get to the spa, you can always bring the spa services to you. You can either have a service provider come where you are or you can perform the services yourself. Now, I'm really big on all three, but it's totally what works for you. I will say that actually getting out and being in the presence of a day-spa will put you in a totally different mindframe than being at home or doing it yourself. It's all about the ambiance, right? If you choose to do a service yourself (DIY), a couple of things you could do is, a mini steam facial or a hot towel scrub. Here is a quick, DIY steam aromatherapy facial and hot towel scrub recipe that includes essential oils (I love the Doterra brand) that you can do in the comfort of your own home.

Here's what you will need:

- 3 cups of boiled, distilled water
- Clean towel for drying and placement over your head (big enough for your body)
- A large mixing bowl
- Your regular moisturizer
- Essential Oils- LAVENDER helps with calming and sleep, MELALEUCA helps soothe the skin, FRANKINCENSE helps with mood elevation, immunity and energy boost and ROSEMARY helps with nervousness and tension.

Instructions:

STEP 1: Allot at least 15 minutes for some alone time.

STEP 2: Boil distilled water and place it into your bowl. Make sure your skin is clean and free of make-up. Add five drops of your essential oil of choice into the bowl. You can also add in your favorite flowers or fresh eucalyptus leaves.

STEP 3: Turn on some relaxing spa music (nothing with words, just sounds of nature) and sit at a table or at your island in your kitchen and place your face over the bowl of steaming hot water and essential oils. If the water is too hot or the oils are too strong, pull your face back an inch until you can stand it.

STEP 4: Place the towel over your head with no cool air coming in and inhale the steam for 15 minutes until the water cools or you no longer smell the oils.

STEP 5: Gently pat your face dry with your face towel and apply your regular toner and moisturizer.

Choose one day per week (I love Wednesday's), set it on your calendar, and when the reminder goes off, start your facial. You will notice how spending fifteen minutes a week can help you to relax.

DIY Hot Towel Scrub

There are many benefits to doing your own hot towel scrub, including…it reduces muscle tension, re-energizes you in the morning and relaxes you at night, relieves stress through rubbing the skin, calms the mind, activates the lymphatic system (especially when scrubbing the underarms and groin), it's an easy massage and deep self-care, can be a special moment in your day (especially if done with candlelight and a drop or two of essential oil), and it creates a profound and loving relationship with the body (especially parts not often shown care; and especially if you have body image issues).

Here's what you'll need:

- Sink filled with hot water
- Medium sized washcloth

Instructions:

STEP 1: Turn on the hot water and fill your sink with it. You can also boil some distilled water and place it in a bowl, just as long as you are careful, as it may be too hot. If you are using essential oils, this is where you add 5 drops of your oil of choice.

STEP 2: Hold the towel at both ends and place it into the hot water.

STEP 3: Wring the towel out really good until there is no more water dripping from it.

STEP 4: While the towel is still hot and steamy, begin to scrub your skin gently.

STEP 5: Do one section of your body at a time. For example, begin with the hands and fingers and work your way up the arms to the shoulders, neck and face, then down to the chest, upper back, abdomen, lower back, buttocks, legs, feet and toes.

STEP 6: Scrub until your skin becomes slightly red or each part of your body becomes warm or your feel the towel get cool.

STEP 7: Reheat the towel often by dipping it in the sink or bowl.

Body scrubbing can be done anytime before or after your bath or shower. Try scrubbing your body twice per day-once in the morning and once in the evening-and see how you feel. If twice a day is too much for you, start with once per day.

Another great way to add to your self-care routine is to sit for at least thirty- minutes in silence or with relaxing music and sip on a cup of tea. I do this often as it gives me a peace of mind, especially while on the porch or sitting around nature. There is a tea for different concerns of the body. Here are a few:

- TEA FOR DIGESTION: Teas that contain ginger, fennel, peppermint, licorice, cardamom
- TEA FOR RELAXATION/STRESS: Teas with kava kava, chamomile, green tea, ginseng, black teas
- TEA FOR IMMUNITY: Teas with echinacea, green teas, goldenseal, rooibos
- TEA FOR YOUR CYCLE: Teas with dandelion root, dong quai root, raspberry leaf

If you are looking for a tea to reduce the amount of coffee you drink, energy-lifting teas are a perfect alternative.

Sometimes self-care can feel good for the moment while you're in it, but when you set foot back into reality, it disappears. What happens when the cute nails break and the massage goes out the window when Lil Timmy spills his chocolate milk all over your new rug? What happens when you've been up all night breastfeeding and you have to wake up early to go to work in the morning? What happens if your teenager has missed curfew and you're so mad your eyes are bulging? What happens if you find yourself in an argument with your husband and your mind is all over the place? What happens when your self-care runs out?

Well, my beautiful mom friend, this is when you REST, ASSESS and KEEP FILLING YOUR CUP WHERE YOU ARE LACKING. Meaning, if you find yourself more tired than usual, that's where you need to fill your cup. If you feel saddened and empty, that's where you will need to fill your cup, etc. At times, you might find that there will be multiple areas where your cup needs to be filled, but that's ok. THIS IS CONSTANT WORK ON YOURSELF. As we go on in this book and you discover all of the eight elements to a healthy lifestyle, you will become more familiar with what areas you need to assess. Once you do that, you implement the area (or areas) in your life that has fallen short; and that is when loving you MORE begins.

This is why I say self-care needs to be done daily and not as an afterthought. Because, if you are filling yourself up continuously with repetitive healthy habits (the eight elements), you will be properly equipped to handle your "self-care run-out".

> *Take a moment and jot down some self care tactics you will implement daily below...*

_____

_____

_____

_____

_____

ELEMENT #3/EMPOWERING PHYSICAL ACTIVITIES

External Physical Fuel

This is where most people want to start when aiming to transform their lives. Not you. By now, you are starting to learn how to fuel yourself from the inside out, spiritually and physically.

We are all too familiar with this element, but yet, sometimes have to be encouraged to do it more or encouraged to not do it as much. With life being so busy more often than not, our physical activities are the first to exit out of our daily routines. 35% of working women reported exercising once a week or less, citing fatigue as the main reason for not exercising more often.

Listen, sometimes you just are too tired and aren't motivated or don't have the willpower to do anything after a long day of work, or just can't seem to get up early enough to do it before your day begins. But, mom friend, physical activity is one of the tools that gives you the endurance you need to withstand work, family, and life. Exercise or physical activity is an activity requiring physical effort, and is another one of the elements that you, as a CEO mom, should be doing daily. Not only does regular activity strengthen your muscles and improve heart and lung function, but it can also reduce your risk of major diseases, stimulate the growth of new brain cells, and even spruce up your sex life. All you need is at least thirty minutes of physical activity to reap the benefits. That's it! One of my mottos, and what I tell clients all of the time is, "ELIMINATE TOXINS DAILY." Toxins are substances that can be poisonous to your body or cause negative health effects. We are in constant contact with harmful organisms and pollutants, that's why it's important to eliminate them daily. Toxins can come from the food you eat, the air you breathe, the make-up you apply, the water you drink, the clothes you wear, and even the toxic people you come in contact with regularly (that's a whole 'notha subject, but we'll get to that later). There are five main organs of elimination, and one of them is through your skin in the form of sweating. Here are my top six reasons to exercise…

1. **It's a form of self love.** When you workout and take care of yourself, it's a way of saying, "I love you." Twice as many women suffer from depression than men; so by exercising regularly, you are more likely to suffer less from depression. For some, it helps relieve depression as effectively as antidepressant medication.

2. **It sets a great example.** The whole purpose of this book is so you can start making yourself a priority and be better equipped to take care of "them." It all starts with you. When the ones you love literally watch you take care of yourself (including kids and adults), they will want to do it, too; and it will set them up to make healthier choices.

3. **Stress Reliever.** Moms who juggle work and family are clearly stressed. According to the American Psychological Association, 49% reported laying awake at night in the past month because of stress. Regular aerobic exercise lowers levels of stress hormones.

4. **Boosts Immunity.** Physical activity temporarily revs up the immune system by increasing the aggressiveness or capacity of immune cells. That may explain why people who exercise frequently catch fewer colds.

Here are a few exercise ideas to fit your blood type:

Type A- Calming, centering exercises, such as yoga or tai chi

Type B- moderate, physical, with mental balance, such as hiking, biking, tennis and swimming

Type AB- Calming, centering exercises, such as yoga and tai chi combined with moderate physical exercises, such as hiking, biking or tennis

Type O- intense, physical exercise, such as running, aerobics, contact sports, martial arts and power yoga

There are many different ways to exercise. You must find an activity that best suits you and your needs. A few examples are jogging, crossfit, yoga, hiking, swimming, JumpFit (my personal favorite, because I am an instructor), Zumba, surf boarding, biking, dancing, and the list goes on and on. If you're starting something new, hold your horses...don't do too much too soon. Do what you can and gradually increase activity as your endurance builds and you get better. I want to encourage you to try new things. Get outside of your normal routine and try something you haven't done before. If you are nervous about trying something new alone, invite a friend. That way she or he can hold you accountable and you all can try something new together.

The number one way to fit in your physical activity in your schedule is to, first, make up your mind that you are going to do

5. **PREVENT HEART ATTACKS.** According to the CDC, 22.3 % of women die from heart disease. Not only does exercise raise "good" HDL cholesterol and lower blood pressure, but new research shows it reduces arterial inflammation.

6. **MAKES YOU FEEL GOOD.** There's nothing like a good ole workout. After a long day at work or a long day with the family, fitting in some time for a good sweat uplifts your spirit and makes you feel really good.

Like eating, your workouts should be aligned with you, your body and your blood type. We are all different and have our own genetic blueprint, but your blood type plays a major role in your everyday life. Your physical activities should empower and uplift you. They should make you feel strong and courageous afterwards. If you are currently doing an activity that you dislike or hate doing, it is not serving you in the way that it should and it's counterproductive to what you are doing. If you are exercising to feel good and to remove toxins, but you don't like what you are doing, you are putting out emotions of negativity. Which means you are detoxing only to "retox." While doing your physical activities, you should remain in a positive mindset. Breathe in positivity, listen to positivity, look at positivity, and feel positivity. If you are at the gym or at home on the treadmill, step away from the world for a moment. Don't watch the news, or your favorite reality show while working out. This is for you to receive nothing but empowerment for yourself. Don't re-clutter while you're trying to de-clutter.

it; and second, add it to your calendar (your phone, computer, refrigerator, or tablet) with a DAILY reminder. When the notification goes off, do it. Don't put it off.

Every single thing I am telling you to do, I do for myself. With work and practice you can achieve empowering activities in your daily routine.

Let's get out of the trap of doing workouts because they are the hottest trend and let's do the workouts that line up with who we are and make us feel good about doing it. With empowering physical activities you will have the insight, perspective, and foundation to kick start your physical evolution like never before.

> *Take a moment and jot down some empowering physical activities that you will implement daily below...*

_____

_____

_____

_____

_____

ELEMENT #4/NURTURING RELATIONSHIPS

External Spiritual Fuel

Ok, so let's touch on one of the most impactful relationships possible, the relationship with self; then let's expand our view to the relationships that we have with others like friends, family, and employees and how those relationships impact our esteem, actions, and overall quality of life.

This element is a little tricky for some of us, as we know that relationships rule the world. Well, I hope you know that. Just in case you didn't know, relationships rule so much so that God created Eve so that Adam wouldn't be all by himself. God said that it is not good for man to be alone. So, if it is not good for us to be alone, then how come it's so HARD to maintain good, nurturing relationships?

As a woman who has often felt abandoned due to the death of my mom and the majority of adults who were held responsible for caring, loving, teaching, and nurturing me falling short, I struggled with relationships for a long time. To be honest, I'm still working on that part, and some days are better than others. Nurturing relationships are simply relationships with people who add to your life; relationships with people who nurture you. They uplift you when you're down, encourage you when you're struggling, they are actively present in your life, they let you know when you're wrong (even though you may not want to hear it), they nurture you... just like we nurture our children. When I was teaching my oldest daughter about dating, I would always tell her that a man was supposed to be like an accessory to your outfit. And by accessories, I mean purses, bracelets, rings, belts, earrings, etc. Accessories enhance, add to, and nurture your outfit, but it's not the whole outfit. And, just in case you lose your bracelet or your ring (whew, it's gone sting a bit), you can still be cute, cause their only job was to nurture and enhance your outfit. Furthermore, you can go to another store and find more accessories that match just the same, if not better. Okay, so from this conversation can you tell I like clothes? You see, relationships are a lot like when I was talking to my daughter about dating. Heck, those are relationships, too. They are supposed to enhance and add to your life, but if they are taken away (again, which is going to sting a bit), you still have you. Your ability to make new relationships are not gone. The key is to focus on you. You can't control how other people act or behave, but what you can do is, control how *you* act and behave. That's why it's so important to fill your cup, first.

A lot of times, our relationships reflect who we are at that point and time in our life. So, if we are constantly growing and becoming better, that's who we attract. If we remain stagnant and never grow, that's who we attract. The problem is, when you grow and become better, you still hold on to the same relationships that reflect who you were. I'm a firm believer in "your vibe attracts your tribe." If you are hurt, depressed, and constantly complain, most likely, that's who your tribe will be. If you are a positive, uplifting and joyous person, then guess what? Positive, uplifting people will be in your tribe.

We were all created to love, nurture, and be with one another; but somewhere along the way, we have gotten lost. It's a shame that technology and social media was created to be social, but yet, we are so alone and lost. When you maintain good, nurturing relationships you…

- Are less stressed
- Are more happier
- Have a greater sense of purpose
- Have an overall healthier lifestyle
- Feel good
- Have more energy

The question is…how do you have nurturing relationships so you can have a healthier lifestyle? Here are three examples:

1. **LOVE YOURSELF MORE.**
   Girl, you are going to keep hearing me say that throughout this book. That's why I'm here. If you don't have a nurturing relationship with yourself, there is NO WAY you can have one with anyone else. I don't care if it's your mom, dad, co-worker, spouse, kiddos, etc. If you are trying to fill voids, have undealt with childhood trauma, or have any doubts within yourself that are not healed, believe me, they will show up in your relationships. Being comfortable with who you are and what you want or don't want will help you be happier in your roles.

2. **GET RID OF RELATIONSHIPS THAT DRAIN YOU.**
   Listen, people can drain you of your energy if you let them. This can include family and close friends, as well. It doesn't necessarily mean that they are bad, but it is good to notice who drains you and why. See if you can transform those relationships by communicating and setting boundaries, loving them from a distance or end the relationship all together.

3. JUST SAY NO.

   The majority of the world has a hard time saying and hearing the word "no." When you say no to things that you really don't want to do, you are protecting your time, while also contributing to a healthier you. Yes, you will most likely hurt someone's feelings, but you are also fostering resentment and regret when you don't honor yourself. If you are serving from a place of resentment, you are not really serving. Period. Every "no" doesn't need an explanation. Just simply say no. Practice with small "no's," first, and then move to bigger "no's." The more you say it, the better you become. Don't be afraid of hearing the word "no," either. You will be surprised by how many mountains you can move with one simple word.

Remember that healthy, nurturing relationships are not always one way. You must contribute, as well. Sometimes, you must meet people where they are in life and continue to love and pray for them as you go. The more you contribute to yourself, the more you can contribute to them.

Take a moment and jot down some ideas below of how you will create nurturing relationships for a healthier lifestyle. Really dive deep into this activity and give it some thought...

ELEMENT #5 /QUALITY SLEEP
Internal Physical Fuel

Sleep is something that we all do, and yet, we're just beginning to understand all of the ways it helps us and all of the factors that can affect it. Let me tell ya, as moms with careers, sleep is hard to come by, especially with young ones. Believe me, the "boobie feeding" nights are currently playing a major role in our bedroom as I write. But, I want you to understand that sleep is a really important element that will help you in your journey to a healthy lifestyle. I love the quote (and use it a lot), "A mama with her rest, is a mama at her best." Listen, this is so accurate and true! When you have the proper amount of sleep, you will be less groggy, have less brain fog, way less snappy and have better decision-making skills. Sleep isn't only important for energy and to be alert; lack of sleep can contribute to serious health issues, which you don't want or need. People who get less sleep tend to be at higher risk for so many health issues such as...

- Diabetes
- Heart disease
- Certain types of cancer
- Slower metabolism
- Weight gain
- Hormone imbalance
- Inflammation
- Depression
- Mental Health Issues

MomFriend...lack of sleep may even reverse the health benefits of your physical activities we talked about earlier. So, there are three main purposes of sleep...

1. To restore our mind and body
2. To improve our brain's ability to learn
3. To conserve our bodies energy

With that being said, here are a few tips on how you can get more quality sleep for more energized and less grogier days...

Try to get yourself into a consistent sleep schedule.

I know it may be difficult if you have young kiddos, but make it a priority and you're more likely to achieve it, and eventually, they will catch on. Seven. Days. A. Week. Weekends can easily throw you off, but by making sleep a priority, your body and mind will adjust and you will be able to properly sustain your days.

Have a relaxing bedtime routine.

Normally, this routine should start at least 1 hour before you actually lay down. Take a relaxing bath, listen to soft nature music, read a non-drama book, turn off the computer, television, and cell phone screens, turn on a diffuser with lavender essential oil drops inside, wear a heated eye mask, and cut off all vigorous activities. This includes running, exercise, and anything that requires lots of energy. You want to prepare your body and mind for the rest it's about to get.

Wear a watch that monitors your sleep.

Thanks to technology, we can now wear watches that we can have phone conversations through and monitor our sleep. Not every night, but wear your watch to bed, and place it on the do not disturb mode. Allow the watch to monitor your sleep so you can see and assess what areas you can improve on with your sleep.

One of the lab tests that is provided for my clients in The Love You More Method™ program is a sleep test. With this test, my clients and I are able to see if sleep apnea is an issue and monitor the different sleep stages as they rest. From there, I help them develop strategies for more quality sleep. If you would like more info on The Love You More Method™ program, I would love to schedule a complimentary Tea & Talk Chat with you. Just simply email info@toyepenny.com and let me know you would like to chat. Now back to the tips!

Avoid caffeine and sugar products including coffee, soda, and chocolate.

Both caffeine and sugar can keep your mind and body more active than you want it to be when it comes time for bed. Choose foods like dark, leafy greens and whole grains for dinner.

Avoid gassy, bloating, indigestion causing foods.

Foods like fast food, hot peppers & spicy foods, fatty foods and even *too much* food can cause gas, bloating, and indigestion. Foods such as these, take longer to digest and will keep your body "working" rather than relaxing.

When traveling for work, (because it is sometimes necessary) creating a space of peace so you can get the quality sleep you need may be a little more difficult. I would like for you to focus on the quality of your sleep as well as the environment that you prepare for yourself in the hotels while you are away handling business. Both environment and quality are consequential for at home too.

HERE ARE A FEW THINGS YOU CAN DO TO GET QUALITY SLEEP WHILE TRAVELING FOR BUSINESS:

CARRY A SLEEP MASK- using a sleep mask can help keep out unwanted light so you can get some sleep. There are plenty of varieties to choose from, cute ones, fluffy ones, plain ones, to the not so cute ones (you get the point) so get the one that's most comfy to you.

USE ESSENTIAL OILS- There are many oils for sleep but Lavender and Clary Sage are really great for sleeping. You can diffuse them, put them in your bath water or rub some on the bottoms of your feet, back of your neck and a little dabble above your chest area.

VISIT THE SPA- Ok, sometimes hotels have the most relaxing, luxurious spas. And guess what? All it takes is an up or down trip in the elevator. Get a massage and a facial and I'm telling ya, you are about to get some good ole sleep.

PUT ON SOME SOOTHING MUSIC- So, after your relaxing massage, nice, warm shower or bath, essential oils in the air, and sleep mask in position… now it's time to put on some soothing music. Nothing loud or anything that would make you want to sing along, but something that's soothing to your soul and makes you relax. Something like the sound of rain, thunder, animals, wind, and piano, you know, nature sounds.

Remember, this is not about an external environment but more about the environment that you create for yourself so that you can be on top of your game everyday for the person that needs you the most, you.

> *Take a moment and jot down some ideas below of how you will get more quality sleep…*

_____

_____

_____

_____

ELEMENT #6/MENTAL & EMOTIONAL PEACE
Internal Spiritual Fuel

As you know by now, contrary to the typical nutritional standards, I hold the belief that the foods you eat with your mouth are a part of a secondary food group and the foods that you eat in spirit are your first line of nourishment. Let's explore your mental and emotional peace to create an anchor for every other area of your life.

A study from University of Cambridge found that women suffer from anxiety at almost twice the rate of men and one study found that about 12 million U.S. women experience clinical depression each year. They also found that there's a higher correlation between stress and mental illness than physical wellness.

With mental illness and suicide at an all-time high right now, it is crucial for you and your family that you are mentally and emotionally at peace. After all, what good would you be for them if you aren't present mentally, physically, or emotionally. Women suffer from anxiety and depression at almost twice the rate as men. We have so many more issues that we deal with, but we mask them so we can take care of others. Mental health affects our emotional, psychological, and social well-being. It also affects how we think, feel, and act. It helps determine how we handle stress, relate to others, and make choices. Mental health and emotional peace is important at every stage of life, from childhood to teen years, all the way through adulthood.

If you experience mental health problems, your thinking, mood, and behavior could be affected. Many factors can contribute to mental health problems, including:

- → Biological factors, such as genes or brain chemistry
- → Your diet and food intake
- → Life experiences, such as trauma or abuse
- → Family history of mental health problems

Positive mental health and emotional peace allows you to:

- → Realize your full potential and what you are capable of
- → Cope with the stresses of your hectic life
- → Work productively
- → Make meaningful contributions to yourself, your family, and society

There are so many powerful women who are moms and juggle careers, family life, and so much more, that are deeply suffering inside and you would never know. Me, I've endured losing my mom, having to go from home to home, being sexually abused several times, becoming a teen mom, being homeless, and so much more. You've heard my story. So many of us had or are having hardships. What are some of the things you've suffered and how have you dealt with them? Have you forgiven and forgotten? Are you barely floating by? Or maybe you have put all of that in the past and forgot about it? However you are dealing with it, I want to tell you that there is hope. You can have peace in your heart and in your mind. No, it's not the end of the world… you can and WILL make it through.

Here's a few tips on how you can have mental and emotional peace for a healthier lifestyle…

USE SUGAR, CAFFEINE, AND PROCESSED FOODS IN MODERATION.

Believe it or not, our minds are connected to our guts. Food definitely impacts our mood. A 2013 study found that the risk of depression is 25 to 35 percent lower in those who eat a diet high in vegetables, fruits, grains and fish, while avoiding processed foods and sugar. It's also important to note that the effect of our eating habits on our mental health isn't just about what we eat. How we source our food, the care we put into preparing it and the way we eat it can be as – or even more – important than our food choices when it comes to our mental and emotional health.

STICK TO ALL OF THE EIGHT ELEMENTS LISTED IN THIS BOOK.

Mom Friend…This is your complete guide to loving yourself more and living a healthier lifestyle as a CEO mom. Implement the strategies so you can start reaping the benefits of mental and emotional peace.

PROTECT YOUR PEACE.

There was a song my grandmother taught me when I was younger and it says…*"Oh be careful little ears what you hear, Oh be careful little ears what you hear"* and then, it repeats itself with eyes and mouth. *"Oh be careful little eyes what you see."* Even though this song is for the kiddos, it's so accurate in our adult lives, as well. Protect what you hear, say, and see. The news, negativity, and drama. That is poison to your soul. Keep it out.

Know yourself enough to be aware of your emotions.

If you are aware of how you are feeling, you can stop it in its tracks. Remember, rest, reassess, and keep filling your cup up where you are lacking. We talked about this earlier with self-care.

Manage stress.

Stress is the body's natural response in the face of danger. Short-term stress isn't likely to cause any major health concerns, but when you're under stress for days or even weeks or months, you're at risk for numerous health effects. Such risks may extend to your body and mind, as well as, your emotional well-being.

Stress may even lead to an inflammatory response in the body, which has been associated with numerous chronic health issues. Stress starters are anything that starts and triggers your stress. Identify what the biggest starters are in your life. Is it your job, the people you are around, time-management? Whatever it is, once you identify the starter, you can then eliminate or reduce the amount of time and energy you put towards it. If you can't identify what it is, try keeping a stress journal and immediately jot down when you are feeling stressed.

Don't be afraid to see a therapist.

Listen, if you are dealing with something and you need to talk to someone about it...Do. Not. Rule. Out. Therapy. Period. Going to see a therapist does not mean you're crazy or you don't know how to handle problems on your own. It means you are trusting someone with your information that can potentially help you get to the next level in your life. Everyone needs a confidant. In your lifetime you will probably have about three (if that). In order to excel as a career mom and be the best you can be, you need someone speaking solutions and positivity into your ears and life. You speak solutions and positivity in everyone else's ears, who's speaking into yours? Get a therapist, do the work and watch your life change. I am not telling you anything that I don't do myself. I currently see my therapist weekly and love it. As a matter of fact, I make a date for myself out of it. After my session, I grab a smoothie and sit to reflect on everything I said and what was said to me. Ask around and get some referrals on a good therapist in your area. As mentioned above, I do want to point out that the food you consume can contribute to depression or other health issues in your life. If you are seeing a therapist and not eating the proper foods for you and your body, you are being counterproductive and therapy will be in vain. Chat with a great Holistic Health And Wellness Coach (such as myself) that can help you make healthier food choices as you change your mind and spirit, as well.

Take a moment and jot down some ideas below of how you will achieve mental and emotional peace...

_____

_____

ELEMENT#7/A THRIVING CAREER...
External Physical Fuel

You have the work life and career that you believe you deserve, but if you are unbalanced and dissatisfied because your priorities are mixed up, what good is it for you to pursue your passion? Having a thriving career is all about taking a deep dive to claim exactly what you want in your professional life and reflect on the impact it will have on your overall life balance.

We have made it to our last element of primary foods...A thriving career. How you show up in the world and serve others is super important as a woman. It's a huge part of your identity and it boosts your confidence, and it's your livelihood. When you have a career while raising a family, it gives you time to be who God created you to be. An individual. You have every right to nurture your gifts and talents, so don't feel guilty for doing so.

When I was raising my oldest daughter Tavia, I was a CEO, when I gave birth to my second daughter Summer, I was a CEO, and while I was boobie feeding my baby daughter Kenza, I was a CEO. The CEO mom life is all I know. One thing I struggled with was trying to balance all of my roles. Giving too much to the business and not enough to other areas of my life and vice versa.

The same goes for you, no matter how much you love your work and family, if you are giving too much in one area and less in the other it can get stressful, demanding and cause you to feel guilty. There's nothing like going to work with guilt weighing heavy on your mind, you will be COMPLETELY OFF YOUR GAME. Having a thriving career as a CEO mom is about being able to confidently serve in your purpose.

When you have satisfaction in your work life along with a healthy lifestyle, you will have...

- Less depression
- Less anxiety
- Less identity issues
- Less guilt
- Less fatigue

Here are a few tips on how to set the intentions for your thriving career and professional life...

- SORT OUT YOUR PRIORITIES. As you've learned by reading this book, you should be number one on the list; but after yourself, sit down and figure out what comes next. Is it your kids? God? Your marriage? Then, your career? Then, ask yourself, "What are the balls that can absolutely not be dropped?" What are the work projects that you need to over-achieve on, and what are the ones you need to under-achieve on? What are the major things that need to be done to take care of your family? When you get clear on that, then you will clearly understand what needs to happen and how it needs to be done. While it is likely that you are extremely accomplished, no one is above improving to establish true balance and harmony.

- DELEGATE TASKS. I know this is a hard one because we like to control everything in the household, but as a career mom, delegating is going to be the key to a happier, healthier life. Since you have prioritized your duties at home and work, decide what can be done by you and what can be done by someone else. Distributing some of your daily tasks to others, and really trusting them to get this work done, will help you focus on what really matters. If you've been saying you are going to hire a new assistant, but you just haven't prepared for them to come on board, then it's time to assess why you believe that you must perform every task in order for it to be done correctly.

→ SHOW UP GUILT FREE. Listen, the kiddos are well taken care of whether they are in daycare, with the nanny or at school, date night was great with the hubby, the lawn guy got paid, and the electrician installed all of the wiring and even troubleshooted the electrical problems at home, now get to the office and do what you do best. No guilt, no shame, just serve. Will things come up? Yes, but if your energy continues to magnify guilt and overwhelm you, health related issues will start to creep in.

When you thrive in your career, you are not only injecting love within yourself, you are injecting love into your family as well. They will appreciate you for following your dreams and it will empower them to do the same.

> *Take a moment and jot down some ideas below of how you will thrive in your career while juggling your other roles...*

Secondary Foods

FOOD AS FUEL

ELEMENT #8 / HEALTHY FOODS THAT NOURISH YOU AND YOUR BODY

Whew! It's finally time to dig into the foods that fuel your body to perform daily. In my coaching practice during the onboarding process, clients are given a blood test, food sensitivity test and a gut health test. This is how we determine their blood type, become aware of the foods they are sensitive to that they are probably eating on a daily basis, discover underlying issues in the gut that may be causing breakouts, weight gain, etc. and then we tailor the right lifestyle and food choices for them based on their assessment. If we find that there are any other underlying issues like thyroid, hormones, etc. we will then test for those as well. Having a custom food guide will be the key to you making sure that you are working with your body to eliminate fatigue and improve your energy.

As a Holistic Health Strategist and a Lab Practitioner, my approach with food is not your average. I don't push pills, potions, and quick fixes… let's get to the root of the problem. Counting calories, carbs, and hopping on the scale daily will just stress you out. And although those things may be important to you, living and eating in a healthier manner should be a fun and tasty journey, it should enhance and add more to your being and not be restrictive or stress you out. My main concern (and so should yours) are the ingredients, nourishment, and if it's aligned with the chemistry of your body. WHAT THE HECK IS IN YOUR FOOD? Although people are becoming more aware of what's in their food, there's still not enough education about the importance of ingredients and how it affects our health.

Secondary foods differ from your primary foods because they are the foods that you actually put in your mouth and eat. Your secondary foods should nourish you and align with you and your body. Oftentimes, we eat just to be eating, and we also eat only for the taste and not for nourishment and alignment. For example, have you ever eaten something just because you were craving it? Then you were eating for the taste, because I'm sure you weren't thinking about the nourishment. What about eating something that made you bloated, or break out, but you ate it anyway? Well, that typically means it didn't align with your body. When we eat foods that are not in alignment with our bodies, it can affect our moods, health, and how we show up in the world. We are all bio-individuals with unique needs that are constantly changing; there is no one diet that works for everyone, as we are all different and have an individual makeup. I like to refer to this as *Bio-Individuality*.

As a CEO mom, food for nourishment is a MUST.

- → It gives you energy.
- → It becomes who you are.
- → Controls your moods.
- → Influences how you think and act.
- → Sleep and so much more.

If you are constantly feeding yourself foods that are processed, unhealthy, and aren't nourishing to your body, chances are, you won't be serving "them" as much as you would like. Believe me, I get the hectic mornings, rushed lunches, lack of willpower, and the unprepared evenings. I used to be the drive-through queen, but listen...

> "Healthy Eating Does not have to be long, drawn out & tasteless"

You can still make simple, quick, healthy meals that taste good and still have time for you and your family. Everyday!

When you are raising a family and serving in your vocation, making meals can be overwhelming, draining and time consuming, Eespecially healthy ones. As you read earlier in my personal story, I mentioned that I resulted to drive through meals and unhealthy food choices because I was constantly on the go and that's all I knew to do. Not knowing that it was contributing to how I was showing up as a leader, mom and CEO.

Working moms have been found to preserve time with their kiddos at the expense of other activities, and therefore spend less time meal planning, grocery shopping, cooking, and eating with their family. We have been found to more frequently purchase prepared foods including fast food and carry-out food, consume food away from home and commonly miss out on family meals. I'm one to tell ya, that as parents, a healthy lifestyle is not only important for our own health and chronic disease prevention, but also for the development of behaviors for our kiddos. My oldest daughter is now 20 years old and still reflects the habits of unhealthy food choices that I taught her back in the day. Something to think about huh? That is EXACTLY why it's all about you.

Listen, there's a conflict between working and family obligations on working parents' and our own dietary choices and strategies to feed our families. We normally select unhealthy food choices for ourselves and for our families' meals not only because they are fast and easy to obtain or prepare, but because they are viewed as a treat or reward to make up for a difficult work day. Outings to fast food or pizza restaurants provide an opportunity for a calm, rewarding family event.

But, MomFriend! It doesn't have to be this way! I'm here to help. You can live a healthy lifestyle, spend time with your family, be a CEO and eat delicious, nourishing foods at home everyday if you'd like.

In order to do this effectively, you must first understand that there are three components to making quick, healthy meals everyday.

1. STAPLE INGREDIENTS
2. TIME
3. HEALTHY KITCHEN TOOLS

By having these three components, healthier meals would be less of a hassle and would create more time for you to spend doing what you love most.

Here are a few examples of staple ingredients you should have in your kitchen/pantry. It doesn't have to be these exact items but use the categories as your guideline. P.S. remember, your staples need to be in alignment with your body, and if they aren't, get something else that is.

STAPLE INGREDIENTS

1. GLORIOUS GREENS

Green veggies are the #1 missing ingredient in modern diets. Learning to cook and eat greens is essential to creating health. When you nourish yourself with greens, you will naturally crowd out the foods that make you sick. Nutritionally, greens are very high in calcium, magnesium, iron, potassium, phosphorus, zinc and vitamins A, C, E and K. Some examples of Glorious Greens would be...

> KALE- Now, I'm sure you know this veggie all too well, but in case you don't...kale is a leafy green that is a member of the cabbage family. It is one of the most nutrient dense foods and there are many different types.

> BOK CHOY- Bok choy or pak choi is a type of Chinese cabbage. It is a leafy green that is connected to white

stalks. It's a great antioxidant, bone strengthener, and certainly heart healthy.

SPINACH- Spinach is a super food loaded with tons of nutrients in a leafy green package. It is great for individuals with diabetes and is good for reducing blood pressure. Popeye would be so proud of you if he knew you were eating your spinach.

2. GREAT GRAINS

Whole grains are an excellent source of nutrition, as they contain essential enzymes, iron, dietary fiber, vitamin E and B-complex vitamins. Because the body absorbs grain slowly, they provide sustained and high-quality energy. Whether gluten or gluten free, the quickest way to create great grains is to experiment and find what works for you. Some examples of Great Grains would be...

LONG GRAIN BROWN RICE- Long grain brown rice is a lot heartier than white rice. This is truly a nutrient rich food. A little note, I'd like to add... The more white the grain or carbohydrate, the more anemic the food will be, so let's stick with brown.

SOBA NOODLES- Soba noodles are Japanese noodles made from buckwheat flour. When choosing soba noodles, look for 100% buckwheat. Compared to other flour products, pasta is easier to digest as it is cooked in water. Whole-wheat pasta contains 4 times the amount of fiber as white-flour pasta. Soba is wheat-free and, therefore, a wise choice for those with wheat sensitivity.

KASHA- Also known as buckwheat, kasha prevents blood clotting. It lowers blood pressure and is truly a heart-healthy food. Get this...Kasha is completely gluten-free and suitable for those with celiac disease.

3. BLISSFUL BEANS

Beans are a wonderful way to add high-quality, plant- based protein to your diet. They are high in iron, B vitamins, and fiber, and are versatile enough that you may never get tired of them. Some examples of Blissful Beans would be, garbanzo beans

GARBANZO BEANS (CHICKPEAS)- These beans have been long valued for their fiber. Just two cups provide the entire daily value. The darker colored ones appear to have greater concentrations of antioxidants.

ADZUKI BEANS- The Adzuki bean, which is also sometimes called azuki or aduki bean, is said to be the most "yang" or warming of the bean family.

LENTILS- The lentil bean is a bushy annual plant of the legume family, known for its lens-shaped seeds. They are a great source of fiber, folate, iron, and protein. Legumes combine best with green or non-starchy vegetables and seaweeds.

4. A SEASONAL VEGGIE

Seasonal eating tastes good and gives your body what nature intends for you to have at that time of year. For example, springtime veggies are light & refreshing. They also balance out the heavy eating that occurs in the winter-collards, funnel, and asparagus. In the summertime, those foods help us cool off in the heat. Cucumbers are an example.

Eating summer foods in the winter can give off a cooling energy; when in fact, your body is supposed to be keeping warm because it's cold outside, and vice versa.

Most people don't know what's in season, and that's why they overspend on produce; and this is why people think eating healthy is expensive, because they are not buying things that are in season. Once you know what's in season, this will stop you from hopping from produce to produce wondering what to get.

In The Love You More Method™ program, a shopping tour is provided so you will understand how to choose seasonal foods and get in and out of the grocery store without hassle. If you would like to know more about the program, let's schedule a complimentary chat! Email info@toyepenny.com to schedule.

PRODUCE YOU CAN'T LIVE WITHOUT...

There are two produces that I believe you ABSOLUTELY can't live without. When preparing quick, healthy meals, these two produces will be your go-to for just about every meal including, glorious greens, blissful beans, breakfast tacos, soups, etc.

ONIONS- Onions are known for reducing blood pressure and LDL cholesterol. Onions have anti-viral & antibacterial phytochemicals and can be used as natural antibiotics. Onions can be used in just about all of your meals including eggs for breakfast, and sauteed for dinner over some rice.

BELL PEPPER- Whether you eat orange, red, green, or yellow, you just can not live without bell peppers. They combine great with onions, too. Depending on the color, bell peppers support the heart & memory function and are rich in phytochemicals that reduce free radical damage. Bell peppers can be used in a lot of your simple, healthy meals including, coleslaws, burgers or maybe even stuffed with a grain inside. As long as you know the more colors, the better.

THE PLANNING/TIME

In order to get the most out of the staple ingredients, you must use them. Say you want to plan the week's dinner using foods from the list above. First, set a date that you want to go to the store, preferably at the beginning of the week. Give yourself some time to explore the health food store and purchase your ingredients.

Second, make a plan on how you will use your basics for the week and stick to it. If you are new to meal planning, you can plan Monday- Wednesday's meal, and then on Wednesday, plan the rest of the week's meal (We are notorious for changing our minds), I suggest getting a calendar or keeping a food journal just so you will have a visual of your plan.

Third, plan your meals using the ingredients above. Your meals can include a variety of ingredients, or just a few. For example: you could choose a grain, seasonal veggie, and a green for one meal; and on another night, maybe you want to combine a protein with a grain and a bean. I would suggest putting a glorious green with each meal, just so you will get a daily dose of greens. Feel free to add a protein with your meals. If you have left over rice, beans, pasta or animal protein, reuse the next day with two or three different other ingredients for a whole new meal. Be adventurous and explore your options.

Lastly, a big secret of mine is to prepare quick, healthy meals using healthy kitchen tools. Healthy kitchen tools are essential to cooking. You will use them daily, for many years to come, even if you are only cooking one meal a day. It is important to make an educated decision about which ones to buy and how much to spend.

HEALTHY KITCHEN TOOLS

Healthy kitchen tools are utensils used in your kitchen that help you make meals a lot quicker and healthier. This is a must for a mom with a career, because it's easier for you to prepare healthier meals at home instead of ordering take-out or making unhealthy food choices.

The first tool is the Ninja Foodi, and it was just released by Ninja in the later part of 2018. MomFriend… this is one of the main kitchen tools we use DAILY in our home. Ok, so not to brag but I made a 1-pot meal in 15 minutes the other day. It definitely came in handy because one of my kiddos wouldn't stop ringing my phone, another was pulling at my leg, and the other one was super clingy and wanted to be held.

I love the Foodi so much, I was featured in their commercial!

I was already a fan of the air fryer and the pressure cooker, but the two of them combined is SO DOPE! If you want to make quick, healthy meals but don't have a lot of time, this is definitely your tool.

The Foodi is an all-in-one healthy kitchen tool that pressure cooks with a crisp. Basically, you get the best of pressure cooking and air frying all in one pot. As an air fryer, it uses hot air to cook your food and all you need is 1 teaspoon of olive oil. So, if you love fried foods but don't eat them because they are unhealthy or you don't like all the grease that goes into frying, this is PERFECT for you! It's so simple and quick, the kiddos can use it. It has eight different functions: pressure cook, air crisp, saute, dehydrates, bakes, steam, and slow cook. If you are in the market for an air fryer, be sure to get one that has multiple functions so you can make many different kinds of meals in a short amount of time.

Second, you need a veggie chopper. I don't know about you, but who has time to cut and chop veggies? I love pre-chopping in the veggie chopper for impromptu meals and store them in the fridge for future meals. It's definitely a great way to save on time. It's so easy, I can chop with my toddler in the carrier. Saving time in the kitchen is what you asked for, saving time in the kitchen is what you get. It's simple, quick and easy to clean. That's about all you need.

The third tool, is a grater. As I stated earlier, a great way to save on time is to pre-prep your ingredients. This grater is a simple tool to help you prepare food quickly in various styles. It evenly slices veggies, chocolates, nuts, etc. I love to grate zucchini for a yummy zucchini spaghetti or cake.

Fourth, a Mega Kitchen Blender by Ninja. I use this tool daily. I love it because it makes it SUPER easy to prepare simple, healthy meals. It goes right along with the Foodi. It's great for making smoothies, purees, toppings, dough, mixing veggies, yogurt, sorbet, grinding nuts into nut butters or queso, etc. Cheers to smoothies on the go!

Next on the list are wooden spoons. Healthy eating wouldn't be healthy eating without wooden spoons. Growing up, we used metal forks or spoons to stir our food; but using forks or other tools besides a wooden spoon scrapes the chemicals from the pot/pan into your food and we can't have that. The spoon you buy should be made of one solid piece of wood with a moderately shallow bowl and flat bottom so that it can stay level when placed down onto the counter. The best feature of the wooden spoon is that it does not conduct heat so it will not get too hot to handle. Always wash your wooden spoons by hand. Never leave them to soak, as this encourages the growth of bacteria and can damage the spoon.

Lastly, you will need at least one good chef knife. Just in case your veggie chopper is dirty, you always need a back up. Plus, it's great to chop veggies the old school way every once in a while; makes it seem like you know what you're doing. I recommend starting out with an 8" chef knife with a tang (the blade) that goes all the way back. Before purchasing a knife, hold it in your hand to get a good feel for it. Make sure that it fits comfortably and feels well balanced. Your personal comfort is by far the most important factor to consider, so try out as many as you like before deciding on one to buy.

Ok, so you have your staples, you've made time and you have your healthy kitchen tools. Now, let's dive into some recipes.

As we go into the section for recipes, keep in mind what I mentioned before...there is no one diet that works for everyone. Experiment with some of them and pay attention to your body. How do you feel after eating it? Did you like the taste? Can you see yourself eating it again or not so much? Because you are a woman on the go, I've found that meals need to be 30 minutes or less in order for you to have time for other things.

Recipes

Smoothies

Smoothies are great cooling treats that can be nourishing, tasty, and filling all at the same time. You can drink one just because, before or after a workout, for breakfast, if you choose, or even for a snack. You can add fruits, nuts, seeds, veggies, or protein powder, the options are unlimited. Here are a few smoothies that I personally love to make.

CHOCOLATE-ALMOND BANANA SMOOTHIE

INGREDIENTS:

2 medium bananas - peeled, sliced, and frozen
2 tablespoons almond butter
1 cup unsweetened vanilla almond milk
1 tablespoon chia seeds
1 1/2 tablespoons unsweetened cocoa powder
1/2 cup ice
1 teaspoon of honey (or any other natural sweetener)
OPTIONAL GARNISHES: Mini chocolate chips, sliced almonds, and sliced bananas

INSTRUCTIONS:

Place the bananas, almond butter, unsweetened vanilla almond milk, chia seeds, cocoa powder, and ice in the jar of a blender. Puree ingredients on high speed, or on the "smoothie" setting (if available), until completely smooth. Divide mixture between 2 cups or glasses and top with mini chocolate chips, sliced almonds, and sliced bananas for a fun garnish. Serve immediately.

CLEMENTINE-COCONUT SMOOTHIE

INGREDIENTS:

    4-5 clementines, peeled, strings mostly removed
    1 ripe banana, previously sliced and frozen
    1/2 cup light coconut milk (sub other non-dairy milk with varied results)
    1 big handful greens
    Ice cubes

    OPTIONAL: Fresh mint or cilantro leaves

INSTRUCTIONS:

Add all ingredients to a blender and blend until creamy and smooth. Adjust flavor as needed, adding more bananas for sweetness, ice for thickness, and herbs for a bit of earthiness.

MINT CHIP GREEN SMOOTHIE

INGREDIENTS:

2 cups frozen spinach (organic, when possible)
2 cups frozen bananas
1/4 cup raw cashews
3 Tbsp cacao nibs
2 Tbsp (packed) fresh mint leaves, minced
1 Tsp vanilla extract
2 cups rice milk (original variety)
1/2 cup coconut water
Sweetener, to taste (optional)

INSTRUCTIONS:

Blend all the ingredients together until smooth. Taste, and sweeten as desired. Serve immediately.

Breakfast

Breakfast can mean hectic mornings and no time to eat. Back in the day, this is when I would go through the drive through to get a bacon, egg, and sausage croissant from McDonald's. Your days should not begin with foods that drain you of your energy, concentration, and mood. Instead, they should start with mood boosting, brain stimulating, nourishing foods that help you sustain your day. Here are a few quick, simple breakfast recipes that can get your day started right.

CRISPY POTATO EGG & VEGGIE BOWL

White onions (which is our natural pharmacy and are known for reducing blood pressure and LDL cholesterol), red bell peppers (supports heart and memory function), and green leafy veggies (purifies your blood and lifts your spirit).

INGREDIENTS:

- ½ cup of white or purple onion (organic, when possible)
- ½ cup of green, red, or yellow bell peppers

1 cup of chopped kale or spinach (organic when possible)
½ cup of sliced green jalapenos
1 tablespoon olive oil
Sprinkle of black peppercorn pepper
Sprinkle of sea salt
4 Eggs
2 cups of frozen tater tots (organic, when possible, as they will have less sugar…I use my local health food store brand)

OPTIONAL TOPPINGS: Guacamole, ketchup, green onions, cheese, salsa, avocado, cilantro

INSTRUCTIONS:

In the air fryer, select the air fryer function and place tater tots in for 10 minutes (12 minutes for crispy).

Place the skillet on the stove and pour olive oil inside to heat. After the oil heats, add all veggies, except for the kale or spinach and saute them for two minutes. Once the veggies are slightly browned, add the kale or spinach. While the veggies are sauteing, crack and mix eggs. Add black pepper and sea salt, then poor them over the veggies and stir with a wooden spoon. Make scrambled eggs. Once the eggs are done, place them in a bowl and wait for the tater tots. Once the tater tots are complete, place them on top of the eggs in your bowl and garnish with the toppings. Serve immediately.

CREAMY, CINNAMON MORNING KASHA

Buckwheat (also known as Kasha) is an excellent source of nutrition, as it contains essential enzymes, iron, dietary fiber, vitamin E and B- complex vitamins. Because the body absorbs grains' slowly, they provide sustained and high-quality energy, which is what we need. And guess what?! It's also free from gluten if that's your concern. YAAAAAS!

INGREDIENTS:

 1 cup kasha
 1 ¾ cups of water
 1 apple, diced (use your veggie chopper)
 2 tablespoons almond or cashew butter
 ½ teaspoon sea salt
 1 teaspoon cinnamon
 Maple syrup (or other natural sweetener), to taste

 OPTIONAL GARNISHES: Almonds, cashews, vegan chocolate chips, your favorite fruit

INSTRUCTIONS:

In a medium saucepan, combine kasha with water and salt. Bring to a simmer, then cover with a tight fitting lid and simmer on low for 18-20 min. Just like with rice, you should hear hissing while cooking and it will get quiet when done. Combine warm kasha and apple in a breakfast bowl.

 In a separate bowl, mix nut butter with 2 tablespoons of water. Blend with a fork until creamy like a sauce. If needed, add a bit

more water, but the mixture should not be too runny. Pour over kasha and apples, sprinkle with cinnamon and drizzle with maple syrup. Garnish with your favorite toppings and serve immediately.

NOTE: If you have leftover kasha, use it the next day for dinner for a completely different meal.

SIMPLE, BREAKFAST TACOS

Certified Organic simply means no pesticides or radiation have been used and the fertilizers aren't made with synthetic ingredients. Eggs are a great strengthening food—they help build up the body, are warming in nature, give a healthy aggressive energy and help to actualize potential. However, you need to know if they align with your body. My body is sensitive to eggs and egg yolks.

INGREDIENTS:

    4 eggs
    ½ cup of onions (organic, when possible)
    ¼ cup jalapenos
    1 cup of your favorite leafy green veggie
    3 corn tortillas
    Sprinkle of sea salt
    Sprinkle of black peppercorn pepper
    1 tablespoon olive oil

    OPTIONAL GARNISHES: Salsa, guacamole, lime, avocado, cilantro, green onion

INSTRUCTIONS:

In your air fryer, turn on the saute function and add olive oil. Add all veggies except for your leafy green veggie. Saute until browned and add leafy veggie. Meanwhile, mix eggs in a bowl and season them, then pour them over the veggies. Scramble and take them out of your air fryer. Place the tortillas in the air fryer with a dab of olive oil on each one for 1 minute and take them out to place on a plate. Add your egg, veggie mixture to each tortilla and garnish with your favorite toppings.

Finger Foods & Side Dishes

Listen, we need nourishing foods and snacks that are tasty, simple, quick, and motivate us to choose healthier options without having to order take-out or go through the drive-thru. Here are a few finger and side food options that are quick and oh. so. yummy.

SAVORY BALSAMIC KALE SALAD...

Kale is a yummy leafy green veggie which is loaded with vitamins A, C, D and E. It is also rich in iron. Mushrooms are great for supporting your immune system.

INGREDIENTS:

- 2 tablespoons olive oil
- ¼ cup diced onion
- 1 red pepper, diced
- 1 yellow pepper, diced

8 oz. baby portobello mushrooms, sliced
4 cups kale
1 teaspoon garlic, minced
1 tablespoon balsamic vinegar (organic)
¼ cup Asiago cheese
Sea salt and pepper, to taste

INSTRUCTIONS:

In a large skillet over medium heat (or air fryer), spray one tablespoon of olive oil. Add the onions and peppers; saute for several minutes until softened. Add the mushrooms and one more tablespoon of oil; saute for several minutes until browned. Add the kale, garlic, and balsamic vinegar and saute until the kale is deep green, but not yet wilted. Remove from heat and serve topped with Asiago or Parmesan cheese. Season with salt and pepper to taste.

You can also add a protein for a more filling "meal" salad, like grilled salmon, chicken, white beans, etc. I also liked having this over a brown rice/ancient grain blend.

ZESTY PEACH SALSA W/ JICAMA CHIPS

Peaches are rich in vitamins C, A and E, but they are also seasonal. Seasonal eating tastes good and gives your body what nature intends for you to have at that time of year. If you are making this recipe in the fall, use apples, and in the winter use oranges, clementines or tangerines.

INGREDIENTS:

3 large Jicama roots
3 peaches (organic, if possible)
2 medium heirloom tomatoes
1 medium red onion
1 jalapeño
Juice of 5 limes
¼ cup minced cilantro
Sea salt, to taste
Black pepper, to taste

INSTRUCTIONS:

Wash and pat dry peaches, tomatoes, jalapeño, limes, and cilantro.

De-pit the peaches and chop them along with the tomatoes. Mince onion, jalapeño, and cilantro. Combine all ingredients in a large bowl and mix well. Transfer to a container or glass jar and refrigerate for 15 minutes or longer to allow flavors to combine. When you are ready to serve, peel and slice the Jicama root thin. Squeeze on lime and serve with salsa.

CRISPY BRUSSELS SPROUTS W/ SRIRACHA (AIR FRIED)

Some sea salts can enhance digestive health depending on which ones. When looking for salt, naturally harvested sea salt is a great choice. It has a grayish tint because it is unbleached so it retains all of its natural qualities. The combination of brussels sprouts and sea salt is out of this world!

INGREDIENTS:

1 pound of brussels sprouts cut in half (organic, when possible)
2 tablespoons of olive oil
Sprinkle of sea salt
Sprinkle of ground black pepper

INSTRUCTIONS:

Turn the fryer on 390° F, and preheat for 5 minutes. Meanwhile, in a bowl, toss brussels sprouts with olive oil, salt and pepper. After 5 minutes, add brussels sprouts to the fryer and cook for 12 minutes. Open the fryer to check and shake 6 minutes before the timer goes off. Keep checking for desired crispness. When time is up, remove brussels sprouts and toss them in sriracha sauce. Serve immediately.

CRISPY VEGGIE COCONUT WRAPS

Coconut is rich in fiber, vitamins and minerals and the same goes for coconut wraps. It is a great alternative to tortillas if you want to use something new and different.

INGREDIENTS:

- At least 6 coconut wraps
- 1 tablespoon of olive oil or avocado oil
- 2/3 cup hummus
- 7 1/2 tablespoons of green curry paste

- 1 red bell pepper thinly sliced or cut in cubes
- 1 cup fresh cilantro
- 1 cup fresh yellow onion
- 1 1/2 cups shredded carrots
- 1 cup shredded cabbage
- 1 ripe avocado
- 2 1/2 cups of chopped kale
- 1 cup shiitake mushrooms

INSTRUCTIONS:

Put your oil in a skillet or multi purpose air fryer and let it warm up for about 1 minute and then add all veggies except for avocado and cilantro. Saute for 5 minutes. While the veggies are cooking, lay the coconut wraps on a cutting board or a plate and add the hummus and curry paste then place in a diamond position.

When the veggies are done, place 3 tbsp filling about ⅓ way up from the bottom of the wrap. Roll from the bottom while gently pressing down and push-in to make the filling stay in. Fold sides in, then continue rolling. As you continue to roll, leave about half to one-inch top seam and spread a few dabs of water over to help hold the roll together.

You can serve as is or you can place them in your air fryer and crisp them for at least 3 minutes to make them crispy. Serve with more hummus or your favorite dipping sauce like sriracha.

Dinner...

Dinner is a BIG DEAL when you are a career mom. You're always wondering what to make. *Do I use a crock-pot or no crock pot? Did I take the chicken out of the freezer? What's really healthy? Man! I only have a few ingredients, now I have to run to the grocery store. I should've planned this meal earlier.* Believe me, I totally get it. Thankfully, here are a few recipes to help you along your journey.

MEXICAN QUINOA...

Quinoa is another grain that is an excellent source of nutrition. It can be used in a variety of meals. One cup of dry grains normally yields 2-4 people.

INGREDIENTS:

- 1 tablespoon olive oil
- 2 garlic cloves, minced
- 1¼ cups low sodium veggie broth
- 1 cup uncooked, pre-rinsed quinoa
- 1 diced tomato diced with green chili

1 can black or pinto beans, drained and rinsed (health food store brand; no salt added)
1½ cups frozen corn kernels
½ teaspoon cumin
½ teaspoon salt
¼ cup chopped fresh cilantro

OPTIONAL TOPPINGS: Cilantro, salsa, guacamole, avocado

INSTRUCTIONS:

In a large saucepan, heat the olive oil to medium-high heat. Add garlic and sauté until fragrant - about 30 seconds. Add remaining ingredients (minus the cilantro and the toppings) and bring to a boil. Reduce heat to low and simmer for 20 - 25 minutes. Stir in cilantro just before serving.

NOURISHING LENTIL & SWEET POTATO BOWL...

Beans are a wonderful way to add high-quality, plant-based protein to your diet. They are high in iron, B vitamins and fiber, and are versatile enough that you may never tire of them. When combined with a seasonal veggie you have a long lasting, hearty meal.

Ingredients:

1 batch lentils
1 large sweet potato, cut into rounds or small wedges
1/4 tsp sea salt
1 cup long grain brown rice
½ cup water
Pinch of sea salt
1/2 tsp curry powder

Optional: Kale, spinach or collard greens, chopped

Instructions:

Prepare lentils. Preheat the oven or multi-function air fryer to 375 degrees. Add sweet potatoes, oil, and salt, and toss to combine. Bake for 25 minutes or until tender and slightly brown on the ends. In the meantime, prepare brown rice by boiling it over medium heat. Once done, add salt, and curry powder. Stir to combine. Lower heat to low and sauté for 5 minutes, covering to allow it to steam and stirring occasionally. Taste and adjust flavor as needed, then set aside. Next, prepare kale by heating a skillet or pot over high heat and add 1/2 inch of water. Bring to a boil. Then place a steamer basket on top. Add kale and cover. Steam for 3 minutes or until wilted. Remove from the pot and set aside. Lastly, prep any remaining serving items, such as sliced cabbage or cilantro (optional). Place in bowls, serve and enjoy.

Toye Penny

JACKFRUIT BURGERS

Jackfruit is a relative of figs and breadfruit. Jackfruit grows in tropical areas of Southeast Asia, Brazil and Africa. While it is technically a fruit, its consistency is similar to that of chicken or pork and can be used as a meat alternative. It is a good source of potassium which helps reduce blood pressure and the seeds in particular is a good source of fiber.

INGREDIENTS: 2 CANS GREEN JACKFRUIT IN BRINE

    1 1/2 cups organic BBQ sauce
    1 tablespoon olive oil
    3 tablespoons water
    4-6 whole grain vegan buns (GF for gluten-free eaters)
    1 onion, diced, for garnish

SLAW (OPTIONAL)

INGREDIENTS:

    2 cups shredded cabbage and carrots
    1/2 ripe avocado
    1 tbsp maple syrup (or sweetener of your choice)
    1 lemon or lime
    Salt and pepper
    Water

INSTRUCTIONS:

Drain jackfruit and pat dry. Partially shred jackfruit chunks into smaller pieces. In a sauté pan, heat olive oil over medium heat. Add jackfruit and sauté for five minutes. Add BBQ sauce and water to pan and stir to evenly coat jackfruit. Cover pan and simmer on medium-low heat, 20-25 minutes, stirring occasionally and pulling jackfruit apart as it becomes tender. In the meantime, make slaw by adding all ingredients, except vegetables (avocado, salt and pepper), to a small mixing bowl and whisk to combine. Thin with water until a thick sauce is made, then add veggies and toss to coat. Set in the refrigerator until serving. Place a scoop of pulled jackfruit on the bottom of a bun. Top with diced onions, coleslaw, and bun top. Eat and repeat until satisfied!

CRUNCHY FALAFEL BOWL

This mediterranean bowl is just delicious. Falafels are made with chickpeas and are packed with protein, fiber, calcium, iron, vitamin C, zinc, copper, manganese, and more.

INGREDIENTS:

Falafel

>1/2 batch vegan falafel (or store bought) In our case, get store bought.

Parsley Salad

>2 cups of freshly chopped parsley (organic when possible)
>1/2 cup chopped tomato
>1/4 cup red onion (chopped)
>2 tbsp of lemon juice
>1 pinch of sea salt
>1 Tbsp of extra virgin olive oil

Sauces

> Tahini Sauce
> Garlic Dill Sauce
> Chili Garlic Sauce

For serving

> store bought Hummus (no need to make everything from scratch)

Optional:

> Mixed greens
> Kalamata or green olives, pitted (if you'd like)
> Pita / Pita chips / Flatbread

INSTRUCTIONS:

1. Put your pre-made falafels in the air fryer for about 10 minutes (12 minutes if you want them a little more crunchy). This can be from the pre-made mix or already pre-made in store.

2. While the falafels are cooking, prepare the parsley salad by adding parsley, tomato, onion, lemon juice, salt and olive oil to a mixing bowl and mix to combine. Then you can set it aside for a moment.

3. To serve, put the salad greens and parsley salad between in a medium size bowl and top with hummus, olives, your falafels and tahini sauce. You can also add some fresh lemon juice and chili garlic sauce. Repeat for each bowl you make.

Desserts...

One thing every career mom needs is a treat all to herself without the guilt of eating too much sugar. Here are a few dessert ideas that taste good and have healthier ingredients.

MANGO CREAM...

Mangoes are a great source of fiber and vitamins A and C. They also contain folate, iron, zinc and vitamin B6, which is good for energy and brain function. If you don't want to use mangos, feel free to experiment and use your fruit of choice.

INGREDIENTS:

- 1 1/2 pounds of mangoes
- 1 lime
- 1 1/2 cups of rice milk or pea milk
- 2 tablespoons of arrowroot powder
- 1 tablespoon of honey or maple syrup

INSTRUCTIONS:

Peel the ripe mangoes and slice the flesh off the stone, reserving some slices for decoration. Purée the remaining mango in a

blender and pass through a mesh strainer. Heat the milk near to boiling over medium-low heat. Meanwhile, mix arrowroot with a little water in a bowl. Remove the milk from heat and add arrowroot mixture, stirring until the mixture thickens. Leave to cool. Combine mango purée, arrowroot custard, and sweetener. Spoon into individual bowls and chill. Serve garnished with slices of fresh mango and a slice of lime.

COCONUT DATE COOKIES...

This recipe calls for dates, which are a great source of antioxidants. They help reduce and maintain blood sugar and are great for an alternative sweetener.

Ingredients:

- 7 dried pitted dates
- 1 cup rolled oats
- 2 cups whole-wheat flour
- 1/2 cup shredded coconut
- 1/2 cup maple syrup
- 1/2 tablespoon cinnamon
- 1/4 tablespoon nutmeg
- 1/2 cup olive oil

Instructions:

Soak dates in 1 cup of water for 30 minutes. Preheat the oven or multi-function air fryer to 375 degrees. Put all ingredients,

including dates, in the soaking water in a blender. Blend into dough. Form little balls and smash them into cookies. Place them on a lightly oiled cookie sheet and bake for 10 minutes. Turn them over and bake for 10 more minutes. Take out, cool, and enjoy.

CHOCOLATE ZUCCHINI CAKE…

This actually tastes like your Aunt Helen's best chocolate cake! Only it doesn't call for as much sugar. In fact, no sugar at all. Zucchini has become one of my favorite veggies. We eat it in my household often. You can make this for breakfast, snack and even for the holidays. Zucchini contributes to easy digestion, improves heart health and is rich in many nutrients.

INGREDIENTS:

> 1 box Simple Mills - Vanilla Cupcake and Cake Mix
> 1 cup grated zucchini (squeezed dry and lightly packed in measuring cup)
> 3 eggs
> 1/3 cup coconut oil (melted)
> 1/3 cup water
> 1 tbsp vanilla
> 1/4 cup honey
> 1/2 cup unsweetened cocoa powder
> 1 cup grated zucchini (squeezed dry and lightly packed in measuring cup)
> 1/3 cup (dairy-free) semisweet chocolate chips (plus more for topping)

INSTRUCTIONS:

Heat oven or multi-function air fryer to 350° F. Grease an 8 inch round cake pan. Dust with 1 ½ teaspoon of the mix and set aside. Whisk eggs, honey, oil, and water in a large bowl and add remaining mix. Whisk until blended.

Add cocoa powder and mix it up, and then add the zucchini (make sure the zucchini is squeezed well, as it will make the cake soggy). Pour batter into the prepared pan.

Gently sprinkle the chocolate chips on top of the batter. Bake for 30 minutes or until the toothpick comes out clean. Cool for 10 minutes, then loosen the cake from the sides of the pan. Place on a wire rack and tap on the bottom of the cake pan to release the cake. Cool and serve.

Hey MomFriend...

Thanks so much for taking the time to read this book and deciding to make steps towards making yourself a priority. I know how difficult it is to squeeze in time for you after caring for everyone else. If you follow The Love You More Method™, you will begin to feel more energized, less overwhelmed and more importantly you will create a ripple effect of complete health and wellness for generations to come. I want you to know that you are the key to a healthy lifestyle. Your next level is going to require more and It. All. Starts. With. You. When you lead by example, everyone else will follow along. Yes, there are going to be some difficult days and even some days that you may not feel like pouring into yourself. Heck, some days you will feel like devouring a deep, dark chocolate cake with extra sprinkles and the unhealthiest ingredients inside. But, when and if you do, it's ok. We all fall sometimes…get back up, read the book, assess where you are lacking, and do it again. You will get better as time goes by. Remember, it's not about being perfect, it's about feeling healthy, happy, and whole within yourself so you can properly serve "them." Here's To Making Yourself A priority…Love You More, Toye.

P.S. Reach out to me and let me know how things are going for you. I would love to be a part of your "Love You More" process. We are all in this together. MomFriends unite, right? I'm on all social media platforms @official_toyepenny. Tag me on your recipes and other healthy lifestyle changes you've made for yourself, family, friends, and society. Use the hashtag #loveyoumoremethod.™

About The Author...

Today, I am a woman who loves who she is becoming. I am a wife to a native of the Caribbean and a Mom to three amazing daughters. I am also a Holistic Well-Being Strategist, the creator of The Love You More Method[SM], The CEO Mom Interventionist, an Author, and a Ninja Foodi Expert at toyepenny.com Whew! I specialize in helping Celebrity & High Performing CEO Moms learn how to put their oxygen mask on first, so they can save everyone around them.

But it didn't quite start out that way...

After losing my mother to Lupus as a child, not having my father present in my life, I was sexually abused, became a teen mom at the age of 16, and involved in a tumultuous relationship with an older man. I found myself at 23 years old in the right place, at the right time to become the CEO of a luxury day spa. I was financially flexible, and I was able to create a great lifestyle for myself and my daughter; but I was also stressed, had unresolved childhood trauma, and carried a heavy load of guilt on how I showed up for my family. Meanwhile my career facade said "I've got it all together". It was my personal life, relationships, and areas of my health that were falling apart.

Now as a wife, mom, and CEO at ToyePenny.com, I have created The Love You More Method^{SM}. This is an 8-step holistic well-being program, that I have successfully used to guide many of my clients who are high performing moms to a better state of mental and physical state of health and wellbeing. In my innovative book, *Love "Them", Love You More*, I reveal actionable strategies on how you can apply The Love You More Method^{SM}, and ultimately model well-being for generations to come.

In addition to creating a method exclusively for leading, influential women who are mothers, I have been featured on Ninja Foodi, WFAA Channel 8, CEO Mom Magazine, and Glamour Magazine to name a few. I am the only Holistic Well-Being Strategist that serves as a CEO Mom Interventionist, and uses The Love You More Method^{SM} as a guide to assist successful mom leaders with their well-being while they fulfill their life's purpose.

In my practice, I privately guide my clients through my 8-step Love You More Method^{SM}, which includes my exclusive one-on-one support, a complete transformational experience, four lab tests, and a Ninja Foodi all in one multi-cooker. The Love You More Method^{SM} is for CEO moms who need to take themselves beyond self care, and make their well-being a priority. It's a holistic well-being and transformational program that will engage and inform you on HOW to re-define your priorities for well-being mentally, physically, spiritually, emotionally and nutritionally.

Listen, 2020 was rough. Women who were once healthy are now struggling with their well-being and their lives. While these women are still running successful companies, managing their households, and homeschooling their children…addictions, mental health, suicides, and stress eating are up by 1000%. The pandemic pushed many of us to our breaking point. If you are one tantrum away from losing your mind, if you have been relying on the wine a little heavier lately, if you are depressed, if you haven't been bringing your "A" game in your company because you don't have enough energy, AND you've been struggling with your complete well-being...I have a solution.

If you are ready to put your oxygen mask on first, and move BEYOND self-care so you can model well-being for generations to come, I would love to schedule a complimentary CEO Mom Intervention chat with you. Send me an email at info@toyepenny.com with the subject line "CEO Mom Intervention" and let's get you on my calendar. Excited to Chat!

www.ingramcontent.com/pod-product-compliance
Lightning Source LLC
Chambersburg PA
CBHW061201070526
44579CB00009B/84